WINNING THE "HEAD" GAME...
Key to Athletic Success
Revised Edition

Sonny Smith
and
Lou Vickery

Sonny Smith and Lou Vickery

WINNING THE "HEAD" GAME...

Key to Athletic Success
Revised Edition

Sonny Smith
and
Lou Vickery

Copyright©2024
By Upword Press, LLC.

ISBN: 9798337690766

In editing the quotes, our mission has been to maintain the original intent of the messages, with variations to fit a sports theme. Those messages that are in italics are personal to the authors. While we have used our best efforts in preparing this book, we do not represent the content's accuracy or completeness. This content may be partly copied without specific permission when used only in a not-for-profit context. For other uses, permission in writing is required via email to the email address below.

Upword Press, LLC
Fairhope, AL 36532

Upwordpress6@gmail.com

Lou Vickery Library
http://Awiseword.life/library

ADVANCE ACCLAIM FOR WINNING THE "HEAD" GAME

"While ***WINNING THE "HEAD" GAME*** is a sports book, it has applications for real-life learning. There is little difference between sports and life--at the end of one is the beginning of the other."
-Chuck Ghigna a.k.a. Father Goose

"I was a head coach in high school football for forty-one years. My team won 321 games. My 1988 team at Pine Forest High School in Pensacola was the USA Today National Champion. I know something about motivation...and this book does the job of detailing motivation and inspiration. Every coach should have a copy."
-Carl Madison, Hall of Fame Football Coach, Florida and Alabama

"***WINNING THE "HEAD" GAME*** is designed to provide a spark when one is needed. The words found here will instruct... inform... inspire athletes to reach beyond their grasp and, hopefully, snag onto something that will improve their careers."
-Floyd Adams, Hall of Fame Baseball Coach, Florida

"It has been 60 years since I pitched in the Major Leagues. I am surprised that most chapters in WINNING THE "HEAD" GAME are ageless. The advice still applies to any age. Don't stop improving and growing post-sports through career, family, and retirement. The book is inspirational and informative without lecturing. It says it exactly right! Well done. I highly recommend it.
Bill Wakefield, MLB Pitcher, California

"In my forty-plus years of coaching from junior high school to college, **WINNING THE "HEAD" GAME** is the most informational sports book I've ever run across...It is a great book for coaches and players at any level of play."
-Alan Young, high school football coach, Colorado

"This, just plain and simple, is a great book. It has more inspiring messages in it than any book of its kind I have ever picked up. I highly recommend it to youth program coaches and athletics."

-Bev Mathis-Swift, Soccer Mom, Virginia

"WINNING THE 'HEAD' GAME is one of the most complete, thorough, and detailed discussions of one of sports and life's greatest challenges! I call it The Mental Game on "The Sports Doctor" radio show. It was always a top subject that Lou and I would discuss in my monthly guest spots on his "Lou in the Morning" radio show! Coach Sonny and Lou have put together a real gem here--so valuable for athletes, sports parents, and coaches at all ages and performance levels!"

Dr. Bob Weil, host of the nationally syndicated radio show, "The Sports Doctor"

WINNING THE "HEAD" GAME hits so many nails on the head that it would be difficult to pick out just one nail to comment on. The reader can easily read segments when time avails itself and come away with a quick reminder. Great stuff that will be either new to the reader or a reminder of things they may have forgotten. A must-read for anyone associated with youth sports.

-Aubrey Whitaker, Retired Coach, Florida

"As a human relations specialist, active amateur tennis player /teaching pro, and overall sports psychology "sponge," it takes a lot to grab and keep my attention. This book does it! Coach Sonny and Lou have employed one of Zig Ziglar's favorite analogies; they have "primed the pump" for the reader…for me! I want more! Thank you, Lou and Sonny, for a great job!"

Wendall Walker, Elite Tennis Instructor, Florida

OTHER BOOKS BY LOU STILL IN PRINT

A TOUCH OF GRAY...Upword Press, LLC, 2001, 2016

TRAVELING TIPS ALONG SUCCESS ROAD
Upword Press, LLC, 2006

THE RISE OF THE POARCH BAND OF CREEK INDIANS,
Upword Press, LLC. 2009

THE LAUGH, GIGGLE, GRIN, AND THINK BOOK
Upword Press, LLC, 2010

NOTES FROM GOD
Upword Press, LLC 2011

GOOD STUFF FOR THE JOURNEY...
Upword Press, LLC, 2012

CHARLIE GETS ANOTHER PUPPY
NXTGen Interactive Publishing, Inc. 2015

REACH BEYOND...Find Your Path to Success
Indigo Publishing, Inc. 2020

ALABAMA CREEK INDIANS...
Upword Press, LLC 2021

HELLO! LET'S TALK!!
Upword Press, LLC 2023

KEY TO SALES SUCCESS...
WINNING THE HEAD GAME
-Upword Press, LLC 2024

For Details:
http://awiseword.life/library

Also available where books are sold

THE LINEUP

1. Prologue...7
2. All About Attitude..9
3. Believe in You..21
4. Language of Winners...31
5. Be Goal-Oriented...39
6. Learning Powers the Future................................47
7. A Will to Prepare...55
8. Spread Your Wings..61
9. Play to Win..65
10. Winning Traits..75
11. Hanging Tough...94
12. Fail (Lose) Forward...103
13. Emotional Control...117
14. A Healthier You...125
15. Preventing Sports Injuries.................................134
16. Knit-Tight Locker Room...................................139
17. Epilogue...156

    APPENDIX (All About Winning)....................157

    Acknowledgments..165

Chapter One

PROLOGUE

We are excited that you have chosen to read WINNING THE "HEAD" GAME...KEY TO ATHLETIC SUCCESS. Whatever connected us, we are thankful we can share this time together.

Why is this the best book of its kind for young athletes ages 10 to 18? The reason is simple enough: The focus is on what to expect during play, not how to play.

Athletic success is not solely determined by talent and abilities. Thoughts, attitudes, and beliefs play a crucial role in realizing potential. WINNING THE "HEAD" GAME primarily aims to strengthen the young athlete's understanding of the role mental, emotional, and psychological factors play in being a champion athlete.

What qualifies us to write such a book? We have 60-plus years of playing and coaching experience, which creates a background that makes the content of this book come alive. We do not write from theory; we have been in the arena.

What is the mission we want to accomplish in WINNING THE HEAD GAME...KEY TO ATHLETIC SUCCESS? It is to apply our know-how and experience to create a deep-felt desire on your part to explore in greater depth what it takes to become the athlete you may have only dreamed of becoming.

We didn't write WINNING THE HEAD GAME...KEY TO ATHLETIC SUCCESS for athletes based on their present athletic status and boundaries. We would venture that you see yourself capable of doing many things very well, athletically speaking. Some other things you do okay, and probably a few are not so good.

We sense that you have something unfinished by being here—something you believe can be much more significant in your athletic journey. Becoming a top-notch athlete is a developmental process. Our purpose is to help you move from potential to reality. Our goal is to provide the ingredients to help you build a bridge from where you are to where you want to be as an athlete.

A real plus at the end of several chapters is a SONNY MOMENT the Coach offers. They consist of the right mix of wisdom and relevant points of interest. There's plenty here for both coaches and athletes. Coaches, in particular, will find some messages by Sonny to offer a unique perspective.

WINNING THE "HEAD" GAME is a resource book. It was not written to be read in one sitting. Instead, it is a book where you can read a particular chapter, or portion of a chapter, at any time that might apply to your circumstances.

The one thing that sets this book apart is that the lessons learned will continue on the athletic field. They have carryover value for real life. They will help any young person who is *"aspiring to reach new heights of success"*—whether in sports or life.

A commitment to reading regularly is essential. So, we encourage you to keep the book handy. See in your mind's eye the energy and power that can arise when you visualize the significance of what you read and put it to use. It does matter how you look at yourself. You must truly believe you want to make a difference in your athletic future. We wish to help you view the unseen possibilities yet to come in your career.

Let us emphasize again our desire to help you nurture your potential…stretch your limits, and work with the gifts that make you uniquely who you are. This allows our message to connect with you, tap into your uniqueness, and cultivate your infinite potential.

Good luck…and great success to you and your team!

Coach Sonny Smith and Lou Vickery.

Chapter Two

ALL ABOUT ATTITUDE

Nothing has been written about, talked about, or discussed more about the importance of success in athletics than this mental state called attitude. Every activity you engage in daily calls for thinking, choosing, and acting. Everything you think, every decision you make, and every course of action you take is influenced, either directly or indirectly, by your attitudes. Authentically, *"You are your attitudes...and your attitudes are you."*

"Okay," you might ask, *"I see that this attitude thing is important, but what exactly is an attitude?"* We define attitude as a predisposition to think positively or negatively about the circumstances, events, situations, and people you encounter daily.

After making these decisions over time, deciding how to react to the same stimuli in your environment takes little conscious effort. In essence, you have created a habit. So, in the beginning, you make your attitudes, and those same attitudes develop habits. Then, in the end, both your attitudes and habits create you. Wrap your hands around that!

You can take this to the bank; athletic success begins with your overall attitude—with what's inside you, not what's around you. Pay close attention to your attitude, which is a critical factor in your journey to be a superb athlete, because your attitude will cause most of the things that happen to you.

While you cannot control everything that happens to you, you can face what happens with a positive mindset. By creating this mindset, things improve because you do everything you can to improve them. You learn to adjust your attitude to positivity. You find yourself doing things to make the best of less than the best.

We want to backtrack a bit and ask you a question. Do you have a proper understanding of what being optimistic means? You can find the answer to that question by gaining insight into what situations in your athletic experience create negative actions.

Managing the negativity that arises from certain activities and events in your sports life is the first step toward dealing with them more positively and optimistically. Take a cue from the moviemakers and "*Take two*" when those negative thoughts pop up. Replace that negative thought with a positive, uplifting view.

Performance Rule #1

On the quality of your attitudes, you rise,
If you are ever to receive the top prize;
For it is true the attitudes you possess,
Determines the level of your success.
So always remember your attitudes rule,
That in any situation, they become a tool
Which determines if you remain as you are,
Or move forward to perform like a real star.
-Source unknown

POSITIVITY EXPANDED

Little can stop you with the right attitude,
little can help you with the wrong attitude.

Positivity serves as the base for building a bright future. It is a life-long task, one that requires almost infinite refinement. Unless you are vigilant and constantly aware, you will not see where to make positive and optimistic adjustments. We will discuss this concept more in Chapter Four, LANGUAGE OF WINNERS.

Positivity is needed in athletics, constantly presenting an intriguing list of demanding challenges. Creating a mental picture of a champion athlete trains your mind to work toward that goal.

Winning The "Head" Game

Converting your desire to be a quality athlete into reality depends significantly on how you employ positive thinking habits. For better or worse, these habits have led to your present level of play and will be the driving force behind your future play.

When you are not playing up to the level you would like and wish to change, any change will begin with a change in thinking habits. You consciously create your habits of thinking, and then those same habits of thinking determine your future.

Experts tell us that over 50,000 thoughts pass through our minds daily—but we can only think one thought at a time. The task before you every moment is to control that single thought. Think about something positive, not negative, about what is good with you and not bad, about what can go right and not wrong.

Studies show that athletes with optimistic thinking habits experience more quality benefits than their negative counterparts. They are healthier, have more energy, make better decisions, perform better, are less stressed, and are more productive overall than pessimists.

However, there has been much misunderstanding about creating and maintaining a positive mindset. It takes much more than repeating many feel-good one-liners (even though they help) to make positive thinking work in your life. It takes a proper understanding of what being optimistic means. It is being consciously aware, moment-by-moment, of what you are thinking.

We humans have the innate ability to adjust and change our thought patterns. We can train our minds to view events with a positive slant with focus and effort. It may emerge over time, but life's trajectory will eventually be pointed toward the positive side. This side will hold you in excellent stead in a sports world tht is constantly throwing complex challenges at you. It allows yoau to mitigate the negative effects of a tragic event or situation on you.

Nowhere is the significance of this kind of mindset more prevalent than in a tense, competitive athletic event where being positive is so important. Your positive train of thought works best when you hone in on the activity and focus on what is going on at any moment. This concentrated effort keeps you ready to consistently perform at a top-notch level, regardless of how events unfold around you.

Please understand that all you need to be great is already inside of you. By continually upgrading your attitudes and habits of thinking, you unleash the innate possibilities within you. Your habits of thinking initiate the steps that lead you there.

> **What does positivity do? Those around you will consistently be drawn to your optimistic attitude and enthusiastic behavior. They will desire to experience some of the excitement that you possess. They will want some of the glow and warmth you bring to your daily activities, whether in practice or a game. They always enjoy being in your presence.**

"The simplicity of thinking in a positive manner demonstrates to others the joy of participating that resides within you. You don't need to wear a sign telling others how you feel on the inside. They see it. They sense it. They know it."
-Napoleon Hill

ATTITUDE OF EXPECTANCY

- Expect the best from yourself, and more often than not, you will get it.

- Expecting to succeed minimizes the intimidation factor of almost any challenge.

- If you expect good things to happen, you become more endowed with a particular attitude that creates conditions that make good things happen.

- Having an internal set of expectations that you can win alone will enhance your chances of being winners.
- By mentally participating in the expectant reality that something good will happen, it will become the direction in which your efforts will take you.
- When you possess an attitude of positive expectancy, you make the waiting period between events more pleasant,
- Good things are more apt to come your way when you are expecting them.
- When you believe it is so before it becomes so, it has a better chance of being so.
- Your expectations can be focused on how you can succeed at what you are doing or focus on why you will fail. Either way, your attitude will contribute to making it a reality.

> **Expecting the best does not make the road to winning any easier, but it mentally increases the possibility. You perform with the exciting expectancy that your very best performance is just around the corner... and it is!**

ATTITUDE OF GRATITUDE

Do you have an "attitude of gratitude?" The more you show your gratitude, the greater the chances you will have to connect with a brighter future. So be thankful for who you are...what you have... and where you are. You will make strides with that attitude.

Gratitude, whether you receive it or express it to others, creates an ever-increasing sense of well-being. You will appreciate your health more if you feel and regularly express gratitude. This leads to better self-care, making you feel more energetic and adequately prepared to perform. Studies have proven that appreciation and gratefulness enhance health.

These studies show that feeling thankful and regularly expressing gratitude leads to a better appreciation of health. As a result, people take better care of themselves and feel more energetic and fuller in any life activity. A grateful heart helps sustain a high-energy thought pattern that connects to sports finest. An appreciative mind is attentive to the sunny side of things, creating more productive moments.

Do you have an "Attitude of Gratitude?" Are you aware that gratitude also helps you to be more resilient? By constantly being aware of the thoughtful acts of others, you seek the positive in almost any situation. This makes it easier to manage and overcome the trauma of any unpleasant experience.

Do you reflect upon present blessings and express gratitude for what you possess? Gratitude turns what you have into enough. You have received many blessings to be thankful for, and the more you focus on them, not on past misfortune, the better you feel about yourself. This puts you in a position to receive more blessings.

Zig Ziglar reminded us, *"Gratitude is the healthiest of all human emotions. The more you express gratitude for what you have, the more likely you will have even more to express gratitude for."*

Acknowledging things with an attitude of gratitude creates a mood and perspective that takes on a whole new aura of positivity. The gratefulness element produces a keen awareness of the value of other athletes around you. Being thankful opens the door for more meaningful settings in building relationships. Gratitude will improve your altitude in sports circles and in life.

The level of enjoyment you experience in sports and life will be determined by what you scatter, not by what you gather.
-Source unknown

Quality results drive us, yet gratitude ultimately fulfills us."
-Roger Federer

ATTITUDE AND RESULTS

Your attitude is crucial to the level of your play. It provides the backbone to a healthy, ongoing mindset toward obtaining the results that help put your team on the winning side.

When you focus energy on the results you want and expect, the brain is treated with an injection of *dopamine*. This is the chemical that makes us look forward to repeating winning experiences. Think about that: A healthy attitude toward winning influences the actions that lead to obtaining those results. Each time you anticipate you can obtain quality results, you will likely be endowed with the resources to achieve those results.

No doubt, a results-oriented attitude will lead you in a winning direction. You will tend to see opportunities where other players fail to see them. A forward-looking attitude will be a guiding light in helping you develop the fortitude to overcome obstacles that possibly would stop less winning-oriented players.

Never underestimate the role your attitude plays toward the results the team obtains. Winning is the accumulation of a team's collective thoughts, attitude, and efforts. Winning is the ultimate barometer by which all things in athletics are measured.

"HEART IS YOUR STRONGEST MUSCLE."

"Excellence at anything requires a heart and soul effort... and you put your heart and soul into action when you perform as hard as you can... as well as you can...as determined as you can...as effective as you can."
-Woody Hayes

The attitudes your heart creates dictate the kind of success that you ultimately enjoy.
"Wherever your heart is that's where your focus will be."
-Pat Head Summit

> Everything else being about equal, probably the biggest difference between winning and losing is a foot—roughly the difference from your head to your heart. Count on it: The 'why' in your heart will consistently mean more to building a better future than the 'how' in your head.

"Staying positive does not mean that everything will turn out okay...rather, it is knowing that you will be okay no matter how things turn out."
— Author unknown

> "There is something that is not always equal during competitive events. Results are not always achieved by pitting strategy against strategy... strength against strength...skill against skill. When competition is involved, events are often decided by an intangible factor known as heart."

"Things that dwell in the heart are rarely curtailed by outside circumstances."
-Fritz Crisler

"If your heart is not in what you are doing, all the training in the world will not avail in the face of strong opposition. Fear drives out all memory of what it takes to resist and prevail and renders knowledge useless."
-General Omar Bradley

What is essential to success is invisible to the naked eye.
-Rick Pitino

Winning The "Head" Game

> **Champion athletes realize performing well can never be regarded as unplanned. Playing well is intentional. It directly reflects your attitude toward focusing on your role, being responsible for doing your job, and always giving your best effort. By sheer determination and willpower, you draw on positive thinking habits that make a significant difference in your play now and as you develop your talents and abilities in the future.**

PERSONAL ATTITUDES WORTH HAVING

- **"My success is by design."** A sense of the kind of athlete I want to be is crucial to becoming one. That's the reason I must have a plan for becoming a really good athlete. I realize that I rarely get more than I plan to get.

- **I won't be embarrassed by my excitement for doing what's important to me."** I will think about letting my excitement for what I am doing bring others up to my level, not let their lack of excitement bring me down to their level.

- **"I believe my 'why' will carry me further than 'how'."** My talents and abilities won't get me going daily, but my desire to succeed will.

- **"What I might consider being no chance may well turn out to be my best chance."** I appreciate that my best chance for a successful athletic journey starts where I am right now.

- **I understand every choice that I make carries a potential consequence."** I will think through all the potential performance-enhancing choices I face and the possible repercussions...and then decide the best route.

- **"I see myself as I can become -- not as I am."** My potential will continue to grow and develop when I recognize I can be a quality athlete, starting right where I am...just as I am.

- **"I will be straight up with myself."** What am I capable of doing with my present experience and skill set? I spend time and energy working hard to improve who I am. Then, I will move confidently forward day by day.

- **"An attitude of curiosity will be my trademark."** A smart move on my part is to tackle the future with an attitude of *"What's next? Bring it on."* I see that as a winner's trademark.

- **"I will be a guiding light for my teammates."** It is critical for me never to underestimate how my attitude can affect my teammates. My positive attitude may not make an impression on everyone, but it will make an impression on someone.

- **"I will always strive to leave things better *than* I found them."** When making things better is my constant companion, I will work hard to improve everything I do.

"Armed with an internal set of expectations that you can function at your best whatever the odds, those expectations alone will enhance your chances of becoming a champion athlete."
    Earl Nightengale

> **If you habitually think about the person that you are, isn't it likely you will remain essentially as you are? But when you habitually think about the person you can become, isn't that the direction your efforts will likely carry you to become that athlete?**

Create a mental picture of being successful. This trains your mind to work at being successful.

A SONNY MOMENT

The ultimate benefit of a positive attitude is that it is a powerful tool in helping players skillfully handle what is required to be highly effective in sports—and life. A mindset is something players always carry with them. It provides the basis of their beliefs and adds value to their actions. Without a positive, optimistic mindset, a primary piece of the success puzzle is missing.

One fascinating thing about the right mindset is you always put a positive slant on any situation. This is big. When you approach your decisions and choices with an affirmative frame of mind, the force of this mindset moves you toward rather than moving away—embracing rather than rejecting--the challenges before you. I guarantee that you cannot think of negative thoughts and expect positive answers.

Through the years, I have discovered that players who fail to see much game action but have a positive mindset can play a vital role on the team. They can energize and motivate their teammates despite lacking exceptional talents and abilities. It is often surprising how much they can contribute without being in the game action.

I believe that athletics calls for a stable and consistent positive state of mind that remains consistently constructive despite ups and downs and normal play fluctuations. It helps a player emerge on the other side in much better shape—both mentally and on the scoreboard. With this perspective, it's easier to make the right decision because a player is always acting to find a way for something good to happen. It is total immersion.

Do you need to overcome specific negative ways of thinking? Making a sustained effort to change external behavior has, as its beginning, changed underlying attitudes and feelings. This effort is designed to act on your behalf and enhance your results.

When positive behavior is the centerpiece of your daily activities, you will eventually bring about genuine internal change. Your positive mindset will beget a positive response to outside stimuli. You will see things differently and react to them differently. This might be the most critical effort you ever make in your sports career—and life.

The way you behave, think, and feel is learned behavior. Being mindful of this should make you more vigilant in suspending negative thoughts and pessimistic reactions.

I want you to know that turning things around may take a while. Whatever steps, however small, you take towards learning to reduce the influence of negative attitudes will make a difference in everything you do. Negative thoughts will pop up occasionally, but you have a choice as to what you do with them.

Just remember that responding to the action around you, in large measure, calls for exercising the sheer power of concentration to look at the positive rather than the negative side of a situation. Participate mentally in the reality that something good will happen, and it will, more often than not.

A positive mindset will help your self-confidence and create a more constructive approach as you tackle your responsibilities on the team. As a reminder, everything you do—time usage, approach to the game plan, preparation, practice, and execution—depends on your mindset's quality.

The ultimate benefit of a positive attitude is that it extends far beyond the playing field. It allows you to embrace all of life--to be fully alive and human. Beyond the world of athletics lies a bigger field to play on, and it's a game that an optimistic viewpoint will equip you to win…regardless of what you do.

Chapter Three

BELIEVE IN YOU

Am I where I am because that's where I want to be? If I am not where I want to be, what keeps me from moving from where I am to where I want to be? Could it possibly be that I don't believe enough in me?
-Unknown young athlete

Are you connected to the best you? Your most incredible value to your future will be in how connected you are to yourself. The stronger the connection to yourself, the better the connection to your future. Wrap your hands around that wisdom.

No matter how much or how little you have expanded. No matter how far you think you are from your goals. The power to move on, improve, master, and experience the exhilaration that comes from being at the top of your game depends substantially on how you feel about yourself and your ability to perform. Can you picture that?

Your first goal is to come alive to the seeds of great potential within you. That's right: within you right now is all the potential you need to improve your base and grow your athletic skills. This potential may be immature and undeveloped—but it is there. With proper preparation and efficient application, your potential will grow and develop. It starts with an attitude. It continues with action.

Your first step is to consciously create a mental picture of how the precepts of what you read here will feel once achieved. See yourself acting on these great sports lessons if they apply to you. Hear those around you congratulating you on your positive changes.

Visualize the desired result. See yourself stepping out and stepping up, refocusing beyond where you are to seek new and greater possibilities in sports—and life.

When the appropriate feelings and emotions come together, you will make great strides in those areas of your career you desire to improve. Armed with this energy and power, you will bring renewed substance to your daily affairs. But you must truly believe in your heart that it will make a difference in the future.

> *"If you believe in yourself, have dedication and pride, and never quit, you'll be a winner. The price of victory is high – but so are the rewards."*
> -Paul (Bear) Bryant

SELF-CONNECTION

Do you understand that self-connection creates the confidence needed to bring a higher value to your external connections? You interact with others on a higher plane when you feel truly confident in who you are and what you are.

What would it take to help undo the layers of inadequate thoughts and emotions that possibly hamper your ability to access a better connection to yourself? Would you not think if you honor yourself more positively, your actual value will show in how you approach people and the openness with which they approach you?

The more you value yourself, the more valuable you become to yourself and others. As you increase your appreciation of your self-worth, you enhance your ability to receive value. Expanding your athletic skills expands your future value.

This journey will not be easy. But with a forward-looking attitude, each step will count. You will grow closer and closer to being the athlete you want to be. Please understand that the journey never ends. You always have plenty of work to do.

This journey requires constantly letting go of the antiquated to make room for better performance methods. The more space you create for something greater, the more you raise your status in the world around you. You will increase the depth and breadth of who you are because you are a more skillful person. Preparing things that enhance your value to yourself improves what you are doing.

The vastness of the unknown called the future is looking for the very best you to tackle it. The best you is the key to unleashing your dreams, aspirations, and ambitions. Are you up to the task?

THE "RIGHT STUFF"

One of the greatest discoveries you can make is to realize that your talents and abilities will determine what you physically can do. Your knowledge and skills will determine what you are mentally capable of doing. However, your attitude toward yourself and your ability to perform will determine how well you perform.

Once you embrace who you are, you have positioned yourself to visualize the athlete you can become realistically. Your mental process then flows constantly toward becoming the athlete you may have only dreamed of becoming.

There is little doubt that many who have gone on to greater heights in athletics have had to overcome some self-doubts about themselves. Most likely, there were times when they had to wonder if they could meet and overcome all the challenges they would face as they traveled the path toward their athletic goals.

But when they were not making progress, they took stock of themselves. They believed they had the right stuff to make it big in athletics. They believed that despite setbacks and temporary feelings of doubt, their mindset's renewed positivity would propel them toward more significant progress and greater possibilities.

These champions recognized that the most important thing they had to work with was what they possessed from the bottom of their feet to the top of their head. They had everything they needed within themselves, and it was up to them to ensure they never lost sight of that fact, even when faced with tough sledding.

Believing you have the "right stuff" will not create new talents and abilities. However, this attitude can help you release, <u>utilize, and maximize your talents and skills.</u>

It's not what others believe about you that matters most...It's what you believe about yourself.

STATE OF BECOMING

We can say without reservation that top-level success begins inside of you--not around you. As an inside-out proposition, you cannot always change what goes on around you, but you can change your thoughts about what is happening around you. You cannot always create a different kind of environment, but you can make the best of the domain you are in. We have probably already said this, but we will repeat it, emphasizing its importance. Just make the best of less than the best.

It starts by creating a mindset where things improve because you did something to improve them. You can invariably adjust your attitude to accommodate the environment favorable to improving yourself and making strides in your growth.

When you create a mental picture of success, regardless of the surrounding conditions, you train your mind to work at what it takes to be a winner. This begins with an internal set of expectations that you make every effort to function at a peak level, whatever the odds. Those hopes expand the ability to play on a higher plane.

If you want to become the athlete you want to be, but you are not progressing as well as you like, don't blame your shortcomings solely on talent and ability. How do you know the extent of your capabilities? You don't!

The barrier to becoming the best at sports you possibly can become has little to do with your capabilities. It depends on the application of all your faculties in building and developing the abilities you possess.

The fulfillment of your desires depends in great part on you discovering the great potential locked inside of you. It is there, and your ability to unfold this potential is always in a state of becoming. So, to become the athlete you desire to be, you must decide to move beyond the athlete you are.

Winning The "Head" Game

Visualize the athlete you can become–not the one you are. This will keep you from putting a limit on what you can achieve. From this beginning, work hard every day to raise your level of play. No price is too great to pay. Remember: Make the most of who you are…for there is plenty of you to work with…and work on.

> **Out of all the possibilities available to you in any situation, you will select one consistent with the performer you see yourself being. Inexplicitly, you will perform the way you believe you can. No more. No less!**

"EXCEPT FOR ME, THERE GOES I"

Numerous years ago, a noted cartoonist for the Disney Corporation took time from his busy schedule drawing the "frames" to a new movie called "Hercules" to draw a caricature of me (Lou) pitching a baseball. It became a most cherished possession of mine.

As a fan of caricatures, I (Lou) have collected many over the years. One that stood out to me depicts a bum sitting on a park bench, watching a chauffeured limousine ease by. The caption reads: *"Except for me, there goes I."*

Those words mean so much because they are so true. They point the finger in the right direction. Who should we blame for failing to fulfill our athletic dreams and aspirations?

Do we honestly believe that other people have more influence over our decisions than we do? Or is the barrier to becoming the person we want to be the person looking back at us in the mirror? Aren't we the chief architects of how life turns out? Do you truly believe that?

Although your environment does play a role in achieving success, you do not have to be at the mercy of outside circumstances. Conversely, you can choose how those events affect your life. Never blame your lack of progress solely on the conditions around you. You hold the power to make the best of anything you confront.

Those who have gone on to greater heights in athletics—and life, have had to overcome self-doubt. At times, they may have wondered if they could meet all the new challenges they would face as they traveled the road to being a quality athlete. But during these times of hesitation, they took stock of themselves. They believed they had the right stuff to make it big in sports.

Despite setbacks or feelings of doubt, they possessed the mindset that propelled them toward better performances. Their mental fortitude assured them they had what they needed to succeed. They never lost sight of that, even when the going got rough.

Accepting who you are is the starting point for improving what you are. If you embrace who you are first, you have positioned yourself to visualize the athlete you can become.

Focusing only on your present state will result in little change. If you routinely envision the athlete you want to become, that's the direction you will take in your sports career; except *for me, there goes I*" is a truism.

To grow beyond what you are, never put a limit on what you are capable of becoming.

"Don't forget: "There are no limitations to what you can do except the limitations you place on yourself about what you cannot do."
-W. Clement Stone

Success begins inside of you... not around you.

> **The barrier to becoming the best athlete you can be has little to do with capabilities. It depends on how you apply all your physical, mental, and emotional faculties to build and develop your talent and abilities.**

athletic dreams and desires, the most influential limit is not what you have—it is how you use what you have.

The best rule to follow is to be explicit about who you are and where you are in your athletic developmental phase. Admittedly, you tend to get in over your head by undertaking more than you can capably do now. Expecting too much too soon erodes confidence and thwarts your athletic development.

What do you hear us saying? How about not letting fear and self-doubt in your abilities grow because you expected to make more incredible strides immediately? Making steady progress is the key to being your best player. Growth for most athletes is in increments and plateaus. That's how you make progress.

> *"Ability is a gift and a challenge. It is something you use, not just something you have…and the more of your ability, the more you realize you have available to use."*
> -William Danforth

YOUR WHY

What is your *"why?"* Why are sports important to you? Understanding your *"why"* keeps your desire high and provides the inner drive to keep you going when conditions are challenging.

Write down ten *"whys"* that describe why you want to be a super athlete. Think about the four facets of being a top-notch athlete: **body, brain, heart, and soul**. Do you have a good *"why"* in each of these areas that will highlight why you enjoy playing sports?

Take two young athletes with the same goals and comparable abilities. One becomes an outstanding athlete, while the other experiences little success. Why?

In many cases, the answer is found in the *"why."* All things being equal, the athlete who enjoys a higher athletic success does so because he has more *"whys"* than the athlete with limited success.

If you want to achieve something great in the athletic world, get crystal clear on your *"whys."* Your *"whys"* will guide you through the bumps and bruises of sports and help you emerge on the other side as a quality athlete. Write down at least ten core *"whys"* of your athletic career. We suggest you do this before reading any further. Do it now!

The reasons behind athletic success are not always reasons that reason can understand.

I AM...
-A PERSONAL AFFIRMATION-

I AM a more unique and special person than I have ever appreciated.

I AM far more talented and gifted as a person than I have ever dared to imagine.

I AM fully capable of growing beyond any performance level I have ever performed.

I AM much stronger and indeed more courageous than my inner fears have allowed me to be.

I AM far more competent in handling difficult situations than I have ever thought possible.

I AM able to generate more inner strength to handle tough setbacks and missteps than I have given myself credit for.

I AM far more proficient and adept in satisfying my heart's desire than I have ever dreamed about.

I AM richly endowed by God with the capabilities to move beyond what I am, for the greater reward of what I can become.

I believe this with all my heart...because it is true.

Chapter Four

LANGUAGE OF WINNERS

*Be careful how you talk to yourself,
because someone important is listening!*

One of the first steps in having a solid belief in yourself rests upon the most straightforward strategy. If you stick with it, using it over and over, it is a strategy that you are almost sure to have a solid abiding belief in yourself. That simple strategy is to always speak the language of winners to yourself about yourself.

Talking negatively to oneself is a widespread habit. We tend to be our toughest critics, and this is prominent when we attempt to give ourselves a boost at what we are doing. We want to be more efficient and effective today than we were yesterday. But often, we are tougher on ourselves than actual conditions would warrant.

Do you tend to be your harshest critic? Do you challenge yourself more than conditions would merit? Do you try to "motivate" yourself by tearing yourself down rather than building yourself up?

When you talk yourself "down," you tend to focus on what you are doing wrong or feel incapable of doing. As a result, you keep your faults and flaws front and center in your mind. You have focused on a negative "you."

In this desire to "motivate" yourself to perform better, you are tearing yourself down rather than building yourself up. Privately, you tell yourself, *"I'm not good at this..."* or *"I'm not good at that..."* And the more you tell yourself you are not good at something, the more convinced you will become. Reality will, in kind, reflect this.

You might say, *"I really don't mean these things I am saying to myself about myself."* Seldom do you really "mean" them. But isn't there an inherent problem here?

Self-talk has a way of becoming a self-fulfilling prophecy. Each time you express a negative statement to yourself, you take a step forward in getting good at being harmful to yourself. You poison yourself without giving much thought to its future consequences.

When the focus of self-talk is slanted toward the negative side, you tend to talk to yourself about what you shouldn't be doing or believe you are incapable of doing. You cannot talk negatively with yourself and expect positive solutions. The mind doesn't work that way.

SELF-TALK BASE

How you perform always will be consistent with what you think. And what you think is influenced mainly by what you tell yourself about your ability to perform and the confidence you express to achieve results.

Without the support of your self-talk, it is tough to perform at a high level. Action on the outside consistently follows action on the inside. You probably innately know that. However, it is common to underestimate how your self-talk affects personal success continually. The secret is to strive for accurate and realistic inner conversations with yourself.

You can challenge the erroneous assumptions and beliefs you have developed about yourself from this base over time. Then, you can follow the path of the new and more accurate inner messages.

Is this self-talk aconcern of yours? Do you tend to talk negatively to yourself about yourself? I think you realize the importance of what your "inner voice" is saying. I believe you recognize that you cannot talk with yourself in negative terms and expect affirmative results. If it is something you need to work on, now is the time to establish a plan for improving your self-talk.

MONITOR YOUR SELF-TALK

It would help if you mustered as much mental muscle as humanly possible to correct self-talk. This is crucial to maximizing and fulfilling opportunities. It takes a lot of focus and discipline to change old self-talk patterns and attitudes. Yet, it is possible to turn the unfamiliar into the familiar.

Changing your self-talk habits begins with monitoring your self-talk. Listen to yourself, notably when facing a tense or stressful situation—often within a problematic or intense event

In this process, you are working toward two very different goals: First, learn what situations tend to trigger negative comments. Ask yourself, *"What am I telling myself about this particular situation that is negative and self-defeating?"*

Second, the goal is to effectively change your inner dialogue to fit a more upbeat direction. The *"Take two"* technique in making movies is a great tool. When you slip up and talk negatively about yourself, simply back up and mentally tell yourself to strike it from the record...and begin anew.

Being aware of what you are saying to yourself about yourself is the beginning of refining your self-talk and establishing a greater belief in yourself. Once you take this first step, you are well on your way to making key adjustments to your self-talk patterns. Focus. Focus. Focus. That is the key.

Fueled by the thrust of this positive approach, you begin to make strides in improving your self-talk...and your performance. You may feel strange or uncomfortable talking to yourself differently, but it gets easier and more accessible. As you do this, be aware that you will shock the old programming in your subconscious mind. It is not accustomed to all those wonderful new descriptions. But it can learn.

Any way you look at it, when you talk in a positive, upbeat way to yourself about yourself, everything else will have a way of taking care of itself. So here is my suggestion: For the next twenty-one days, consciously focus on speaking *"up words."* Tell yourself what is right with you – not what is wrong; what you can do -- not what you can't do...What you want to happen, not what you don't want to happen. Dwell on your "plusses", not your "minuses." Employ best self-talk to lift yourself up, not put yourself down.

Your self-talk has been the catalyst to where you are and will be the force behind where you go. Without the support of your self talk, it will be extremely difficult to perform at a high level.

SELF-TALK "MUSTS"

- **Keep a close tab on your "apostrophe tees."** You know the ones I am talking about: can't, won't, shouldn't do, wouldn't do, and don't want to do. The more you use these in a personal sense, the more negative you become. Work to eliminate as many apostrophe tees from your self-talk as possible.

- **Don't tie yourself in "nots."** If you persist in using self-defeating statements, they become a self-fulfilling prophecy. Eliminate the "nots" for the more you tell yourself that you are not good at doing something, the more convinced you become. Untie these "nots" in your self-talk:

    The can nots…
     The may nots…
      The would nots…
       The do nots…
        The will nots…
         The could nots…
          The should nots…
           The am nots

Mostly watch the use of the "am nots," like *"I am not good enough."* Sure you are!

- ***"What if."*** Do you say things like: *"If I were this, I would be better at that,"* or *"If I had that, I would be better at this?"* *"What if"* statements never make you better. They are success-stoppers and impede your progress.

- **Get off your *"buts."*** You cannot keep up with the changes around you if "*Yes, but...*" becomes your hallmark. Listen to how often you tell others why you can or will do something, then in the next breath, offer a "but" followed by all the reasons why you cannot. It's amazing how everything is said before *but* has little or no significance.

- Here is the positive step. Learn to use the *"in the bag"* concept. Whatever you want to change or improve, state it in the present tense as if it is an accomplished fact. Make your self-talk statements like: "I am...", "I have...", and "I do...". Using this kind of language long enough and persistently it becomes ingrained in your belief system.

STATEMENTS TO ELIMINATE

Numerous statements about oneself are used, which add nothing to improving one's life. They take away from the positivity needed when facing a difficult life challenge. These statements would include:

- "If I had only..."
- "It's not fair"...
- "This is too complicated"...
- "Why does this have to be so challenging"...?
- "I have to do that?"...
- "Why is this happening to me?"

Countless other "negative" statements are used when talking to ourselves. None of these statements offers any motivation to seek solutions. They add to the excuse list. We called this a "loser's limp." It is quite common in sports.

Now, go back over the list of statements at the top and put a positive slant on each. For example, instead of *"Why is this happening to me?"* Use something like this: *"What can I learn from this situation?"* Another one could be, *"How can I make this fair?"* Just attempt to focus on how you can make it positive.

There is an important reason why you must consciously think about what you are saying to correct how you speak to yourself. The *"Subconscious mind"* is listening to every word spoken.

Being okay with what you tell yourself you are is the starting point for improving what you are.

THE SUBCONSCIOUS MIND

Remember that everything good will not happen at a moment's notice. If what the subconscious mind has been hearing has been negative, instant miracles cannot be expected. As the reactive mind, the subconscious tends to be skeptical when the conscious mind proposes a change in thinking and acting.

For example, the subconscious mind will react like this: *"Hold on now, who are you trying to fool with all this positive stuff? I'll believe it when I see it!"* Remember from a previous discussion how it will take about 21 days to make it a daily, ongoing reality.

It will take those three weeks for all the positive thoughts planted in the subconscious mind to be awakened. Then the subconscious one day will say, *"Gosh, you're right about this positive stuff...and I like what I'm hearing."* Okay. That's probably a stretch, but the result isn't.

To be habitually successful, keep talking with yourself positively and upbeat. Repeat these kinds of affirmations to yourself long and powerfully enough so that they eventually register in the far recesses of the subconscious mind.

"Positive, upbeat language spoken persistent enough to yourself will eventually become a part of your belief system."
-Dr. John Maxwell

Winning The "Head" Game

If you believe, talk and act like a winner,
you have an excellent chance of being a winner;
If you believe, talk, and act like a loser,
you have an excellent chance of being a loser.

UNFOLD POTENTIAL

Unfolding potential begins with focusing on your strengths, rather than on your limitations...on the reasons why you can succeed--not on what might hold you back. When you tell yourself that you can be the successful athlete your vision tells you can become, that's when you reach out toward the future and do things you have only dreamed of doing, things you might have thought that you could not even possibly do.

Talk to yourself as if you
are what you want to be.

Without the support of your positive self-talk, it is tough to perform at a high level. Action on the outside consistently follows action on the inside. You probably innately know that, but it is easy to underestimate the power self-talk has on personal success continually. Is this something you need to work on going forward?

Anything we do results from what we think and believe is influenced mainly by what we tell ourselves about our capacity. That's the bottom line.

> You are what you tell yourself you are;
> You do what you tell yourself you can do;
> You become what you tell yourself you can become;
> You generally get what you tell yourself you deserve.
> -Source unknown

You cannot lift yourself up by talking yourself down.

SELF-TALK GUIDELINES

- **PRACTICE "MIRROR TALK."** Start the day right. Recite positive things about yourself before you start your day. Do it until it sounds like you really mean what you say.

- **"TAKE TWO."** When a mistake is made while shooting a scene, movie makers say, "*Take two*," and repeat it. Use the "*Take two*" technique to help you unlearn old self-talk habits until they become part of your belief system.

- **USE THE PRESENT TENSE.** (A reminder of something earlier) Start your self-talk with statements like: "*I am...*" or "*It is...*"— ones that express things as if they are already accomplished.

- **KEEP YOUR SELF-TALK SIMPLE.** Painting word pictures to yourself improves your ability to act on your inner suggestions. Simple words paint the clearest word pictures.

- **BE PRACTICAL.** Whatever you expect, don't expect immediate miracles in improving your self-talk habits. Learning new self-talk principles takes time and patience.

- **BE SPECIFIC.** When talking with yourself, don't beat around the bush. Be straightforward with yourself about what needs to be done. Vague self-talk leads to ambiguous results.

Chapter Five

BE GOAL-ORIENTED

"A goal is a vision about where you would like to be at some point in the future."
-Jim Rone

All action in sports occurs in terms of movement. The key factor behind all movement of any consequence is motivation. Motivation in the sports world can be described as a psychological driving force that arouses or reinforces action toward the desired goal of performing at peak capacity and creating opportunities for winning. Motivation evolves around both internal and external factors.

External motivation serves a role in moving athletes to action through the offering of awards and rewards. Unquestionably, winning the trophy can be a motivating goal. However, internal motivation factors move the needle in the long run.

Internal motivation is a product of our purpose, values, and beliefs. It is the driving force behind seeing just how good we can be. Internal motivation is the only motivation that is sustained through tough times and external stimuli that affect progress. The strength to become the best arises from internal motivation, where you do not feel the need to depend on outer incentives of any kind to get you going.

Internal motivation is the nature of motivation where you find its place in those goals you set for yourself. Motivational goals are genuinely personal and rarely rise above the level where you set them. To soar high, sow big. And as Mark Twain once said, *"If you aim high enough, you won't shoot yourself in the foot."*

Internal motivation tends to work its way over and through goals that may appear uncomfortable to achieve initially. But once you get in the mix of working toward fulfilling those goals, they become even more significant motivators.

Another critical factor in motivational goals is whether the sport you play allows you to distribute your talents best. Are you doing what you genuinely enjoy in an environment where you genuinely enjoy doing it? Your talents must be congruent with your sport. So, find a locker room that aligns with yours and set your goals accordingly.

SENSE OF PURPOSE

As your purpose is, so is your will.

As your will is, so are your deeds.

As your deeds are, so are your rewards.

Do you have a crystal-clear purpose for what you want to accomplish during your sports experience? Your road to being a superb athlete begins with a solid purpose around which you build your motivational goals. This is the course you take to aspire toward your athletic destiny. Real self-growth does not happen without a solid and realistic purpose.

The backbone of becoming a quality athlete is a purpose that arises deep within you. With a tremendous underlying purpose, you are more likely to always have direction, your goals are more secure, your focus is razor-sharp, and your potential is more pronounced. With a strong sense of purpose, you quickly and more readily tap into the reserves of energy, desire, and courage. Purpose enables you to connect with your mission and be passionate about it. It sits right at the heart of your soul.

How do you establish a greater sense of purpose in your athletic experience? It evolves from doing things that come naturally to you. Are you able to see opportunity amidst problems? Are you able to come up with solutions, thinking outside the box? Can you step out of your comfort zone and move beyond the status quo? Are you a natural-born leader? Are you a gifted communicator? Are you a problem-solver?

Think of your purpose as being your mission statement. *"I want to be...I want to do... I want to have..."* The answers hold the purpose for your athletic experience. And the most significant purpose is doing something you can have fun doing.

With a true sense of purpose, you will tend to look at yourself--not as the athlete you are–but as the athlete you can become. You will never grow beyond the athlete you are until you decide what kind of athlete you want to be.

VISUALIZE SUCCESS

"The only thing worse than being blind is having sight and no vision."
-Helen Keller

Your purpose has at its very beginning, a vision. From this visionary start, you formulate the purpose of what you would like to accomplish as an athlete. This vision enables you to develop the kind of athlete you would like to be in your imagination. If you can imagine it, you can do it. If you can visualize it, you can become it.

Since your vision is set at the heart of your purpose, it becomes the centerpiece of establishing goals that take you further than the eye can see. Think about that. It would be best to never focus on goals that are easy to achieve. Let your imagination reach far beyond your horizon, where you find *stretch* goals.

The imagination is the workshop where the construction of your future begins. It allows you to explore the possibilities and probabilities that can be created on the road to success. The imagination lays the pavement over which your reality ride eventually carries you.

On your visualized trips, imagine being and doing something special. Visualize your plan to proceed long before you begin the journey. Imagine what must be done to reach the pinnacle of a triumphant destination. Getting from here to there is challenging if you have no idea where 'there' is.

Following your vision will accommodate an environment where you grow and improve because you did something to help yourself grow and develop. It all begins with a vision…, and then you move on to action and rewards.

> **Success at almost anything arises from a vision. It really begins with a question mark that loops around your brain, asking,** *"Can I do this?"* **From that visionary start, you move forward to answer the question in your mind's eye with a resounding** *"Yes!"* **You know you can never rise above your vision…so you follow your vision to accommodate the kind of environment where you grow and improve. Do something special to cultivate possibilities.**

"Goals provide direction. Where do you want to be after you have gone through a series of athletic experiences? A clear picture of where you are headed is crucial if these experiences are to lead to a successful conclusion."
-Jill Korrath

"The road to success is built on a matter of choice… not a matter of chance. If you have no idea where you are going, how will you know when you arrive?"
-Mark Cuban

"Don't worry about trying to get ahead of others… the thrust behind your goals should be to stay ahead of your prior performance levels."
-Dr. Gaylon McCollough

> **Goal setting is like planning a trip: First, locate where you are. Second, decide where you want to be in a certain time period. Third, plan the route to get there.**

GOAL-SETTING KEYS

Set goals just out of reach...not completely out of sight.

- Goal setting is done from the future back to the present. Learn from the past...plan for the future...perform in the present.

- Set realistic, challenging, daily, weekly, and seasonal goals that are desirable, believable, and achievable.

- Set stretch goals, but don't set them so high that they are rarely accomplished. Goals that extend beyond the grasp have the best motivational value over the long run.

- To be effective, goals must be measured by quantity, quality, and time. Otherwise, they probably are not worth the time spent on identifying them.

- Write your goals down so you can see them...study them... refer back to them. This not only gives you a chance to check up occasionally to determine the extent of your progress, but it also creates focus, and what you focus on tends to expand.

- Goals to be reached must harmonize with action. In other words, goals are achieved through daily action plans and proper execution.

- Determine what obstacles must be overcome to reach goals. Then, plan what you need to do to overcome them.

- Goals should be shared with those who can encourage and assist in achieving them. Getting them involved also reaffirms a personal commitment.

- Set a deadline for each goal. Some goals may have natural deadlines–the length of time, etc. But if they don't, set them. Without time deadlines, goals are limited in value.
- Always begin your goal-setting statements with the term, *"I am...I will...I can..."* Think about what the action will look like as you work toward the end goal.

"Goals help capture the desire to extend beyond those limits that you thought possible."
-Ken Blanchard

"Individual goals are born in the heart and mind... and only there will they ever die."
-W. Clement Stone

Your number one goal should be to work harder on improving yourself than on anything else that you do. So set goals that will lead you to being a special athlete.
-Don Shula

> **Don't worry about trying to get ahead of others... the thrust behind your goals should be to stay ahead of your prior performance levels.**

"Any goal lightly set will be easily forgotten at the first sign of difficulty. The moral: Don't establish a goal to just test the waters...set it to make a big splash."
-Bobby Bowden

> **Goal-setting is done from the future back to the present. The only time you ought to be looking backward is when you are searching for things to help you move forward.**

Winning The "Head" Game

What you get by reaching a goal is not as important as what you become by reaching a goal.

"It's just as difficult to reach a destination you don't have as it is to come back from a place you have never been."
-Zig Ziglar

CREEDS NEED DEEDS

Once you have an excellent handle on your goals, the next crucial step is to establish a pattern for achieving them. Goals must harmonize with action.

What is the single action that, if taken, will enhance the likelihood of desired goals falling into place? Establishing a workflow pattern where your creeds mandate deeds is the answer.

The absence of a solid plan to be *"deed conscious"* leads to a tendency to focus on the most effortless tasks. There must be a consorted effort to extend your efforts so you can expand your base. Action must be broad enough and deep enough to perform deeds that reach goals that move you forward.

The more challenging the creeds, the greater the requirement for appropriate deeds. Otherwise, you are just hoping for something good to happen. As Dr. John Maxwell states, *"Hope is not an effective strategy in any undertaking."*

"The road you travel is clearer... your travels are filled with doing more of the right kind of things... the certainty of the destination is greater, when you know where you're headed."
-Tom Peters, Life Coach

AVERAGE IS NOT A GOAL

Have you ever heard anyone say, *"I really look forward to being average?"* Not everyone will profess a craving to be great. Some want to be good. But no one wants to be average. Average is a term reserved for politicians and mathematicians. It has no significance in athletics. Take a good look at these thoughts:

TO BE AVERAGE is to seek security instead of opportunity... to let an endless string of opportunities pass by... to accept the status quo as the best existence.

TO BE AVERAGE is to be imprisoned by the comfortable habit of doing what one is required to do... not what one is capable of doing -- to be less than what one is capable of becoming.

TO BE AVERAGE is never to perform at a higher level... to tune one's receiver to the mediocre frequency and join the pack... to adjust to the standards of others.

TO BE AVERAGE is to be "the top of the bottom, the bottom of the top... the best of the worse, the worst of the best."

TO BE AVERAGE is to fail to expand thinking and challenge abilities... to play the waiting game of hoping luck, chance and circumstance will pull one up to the top.

TO BE AVERAGE when your last breath is drawn, is to have sat on the sidelines and watched one's best opportunities go by -- to have accepted minimal risks and made minimal decisions in the most important game of all -- the game of life.

> **Nothing average ever stood as a monument to success ...for when success is looking for a partner, it doesn't turn to those who believe they are only average -- it turns instead to those who are forever searching and striving to become the very best they possibly can be.**

Chapter Six

LEARNING BUILDS A FUTURE

The talent and ability to develop athletic skills are tremendous gifts. However, athletic prowess must be secondary to educational growth and development. It would be best if you embraced the attitude that education is your ultimate ticket to success in almost anything you do. It is the bridge that will pass the very best things you will get out of life. So, no matter your athletic dreams, obtaining a quality education is the soil in which those dreams do their best growing and developing.

If you are a student, do you appreciate the fact that what you do today in the classroom will be a part of the rest of your life? This makes your wisest decision today, where you apply yourself in the classroom with the same vigor and enthusiasm you have in the athletic arena or playing field. Work toward what you hope to become after your competitive athletic days. All levels of sports careers do end, necessitating preparation for the next part of life.

It is essential to be highly effective as an athlete to leave some wiggle room for the educational side of the equation. Making quality adjustments on your educational journey is a critical factor in determining the level of effectiveness you experience. This creates a need to rethink the exploration of what you should be doing to be more effective in the classroom. Your goal is to always attempt to be really good in the classroom…and on the playing field.

LEARNING IS AN ACTIVE PROCESS

"*You can't teach an old dog new tricks*," is an old saying. How we look at that statement may be true of dogs, but it is not true of humans. As human beings, the ability to learn is not marked by years; a state of mind marks it. As another old saying goes, *"Years will weather our hide, but to quit learning will weather our soul. Knowledge and skills know no age -- they never grow old."*

How willing are you to reach out for something new? Some of the best things you learn will be learned after you believe you have learned everything you need to know. That may not be descriptive of where you are in your personal development because of age, but learning something new and different is a forever thing.

The learning process can start anytime—anywhere…but you have to take the first step; you have to begin. You have to recognize the real significance of the act of learning, regardless of where and what the learning process is all about—it is an active engagement.

Once you have started, your mind will mobilize all its forces. Your whole being will be involved in the learning effort. But you must take the first step; then, you will be on your way—you will grow your knowledge base from there.

Learning aims to acquire ways and means of always intending to perform at a higher level. This attitude will save you time working to improve because a higher level is just one step or lesson away.

It is important to remember that you only aspire to new heights when you are willing to say "Yes" to discovering and learning new and creative ways to perform. Always be a sponge. Learning is forever.

> *"The more you know, the more you realize there is to know. You need to know that you will never know all you need to know about what you ought to know. So, keep on learning."*
>   -Bob McCorkle

> *"Habits decide where you are going…but also take you to where you have been. Learning new things involves unlearning old things."*
>   -Dr. Ken Blanchard

Winning The "Head" Game

> **"Good is the enemy of better, and better is the enemy of best"...and "good enough is not good enough if better is possible." "the best way to improve your good is to work to make your best better." So, "stay with it until your good is better... and your better is best."**
> -Adapted from several sources

EXPERIENCING SOMETHING DIFFERENT

The root of all learning and the catalyst for beginning the learning process is simple. It starts by desiring the benefits of learning something new and different more than choosing to continue the status quo.

The adventurous nature of this consciousness is the desire to move headstrongly into learning. The one thing that never changes is that everything is invariably evolving—there is always something to learn. Acceptance will keep you from doing the same old things in the same old ways and expecting different results.

Learning athletic skills entails a lot of realistic work. It requires extending in the direction of doing what you probably haven't done to add new dimensions of habitual growth to your sports activities.

When you mentally move toward learning expansion, your capacity to change and adapt allows you to see possibilities you have never experienced before. This awareness will enable you to establish a foothold of what it will take to move you to the next level instead of continuing along a similar path.

The first phase of experiencing something different is a commitment to doing something different. We have said it several times: to have it the way you want it, you must give up the way it is. The energy to pursue something that will add immeasurably to your future lies within the consciousness of envisioning how your capacity to learn is what allows you to move forward. One of the most consistent things you can count on is that there will always be something new and different to learn and expand your horizons.

The next phase in the learning process is to follow actively and even seek out beneficial adjustments recommended by your superiors. If you don't change the right things, you can't expect to have upgraded your athletic experience, can you? Just make sure you are advancing in the right direction, for redirection is only a plus for your sports career if it is in the right direction.

Here are some other worthy thoughts on the learning process:

- Necessity has been called the mother of invention. Among us humans, it also can be called the mother of change.

- Be grateful for how something was beneficial to your past efforts. Be appreciative of what your past has brought you. But if now is the time to "let go," mentally prepare to move on to something better.

- Not all performance modifications lead to growth, but there is no growth without alterations in how you play. Change is never fixed or static. It is an ongoing event awakening your internal ability to adjust and adapt.

- The motivation to move on beyond where you are can happen through the benefit of just a simple variation in your training regimen. This modification can get you moving in a more creative and productive direction.

- There is a world of difference between having a desire to improve and having an improvement plan. The more committed you are to a plan for improving, the less complicated the improvement process will be.

- The longer you put off upgrading your skills and techniques, the longer it will take when you get to it.

- It is easier to discard personal responsibility for change than to accept it. Regardless of the needed change, most of us would say, *"I'm doing okay with the way things are; why change now?"* But familiarity is a battle cry that leads to mediocrity…or something worse.

- The most oversized room for any young athlete is the room for improvement. Compete against yourself. Self-improvement is about being better today than you were yesterday and the day before that.

- When you limit how much you expect to improve, haven't you put a limit on how much you will improve?

> **If you keep doing what you have always done, you won't keep getting the results you have always gotten. That's because skills, methods, and tactics must be constantly upgraded to keep up with the changes happening around you…and within you.**

"The importance of learning, changing, and adjusting are key elements in growth. Reaching the pinnacle of effectiveness calls for applying a learning mentality to almost everything you do."
-George Washington Carver

> **Unless you are willing to leave some of your old points of view behind, you will seldom find yourself in a position to create something better-- and possibly more lucrative in the days ahead.**

"Nothing fails like success if it keeps you from learning new and better habits of performing … for to have it the way you want it; you must move beyond the way it is."
-A.M. Williams

SKILLFULNESS

Every athlete needs to upgrade skills--of some kind regularly.

We think the message to be conveyed here is reasonably evident: Constant enhancement and improvement in your foundational skills base should be your standard of preparation performance. The process of skills growth is tied to the desire to want to learn.

Learning is a process. Skillfulness results from it. Skills development is established through learning upgrades that lead to more sustainable skill expansion. The more you know about doing something, the fewer surprises and obscurities you encounter.

Over time, everything becomes either more apparent or suggestive of something else. This, in turn, leads to another possible learning experience... and then another. That is the skills progression you want to follow.

Skills growth is never static. It is stimulated by instructive behavior, which continually seeks ways to enlarge one's skill base and expand one's ability to perform better and better.

The challenge is learning to become highly proficient in the practice time allotted and with the highest degree of dependability. Instinctively, select the correct action at the right time and as realistically as possible under actual playing circumstances. This is the basis for developing, expanding, and building skillfulness.

In our experience, the learning process is best served by being attuned to the originality of daily improvement. Concentrate on making incremental progress daily. This thought progression leaves the obscurities of the future and the boredom of the present at the door. The now moment is always the best learning moment.

Understanding that progress can move slowly when seeking ways to expand your skill base would help. It would help if you appreciated that you cannot conquer everything alone. Discovering and growing new and different skills takes time.

Many young athletes struggle with not receiving instant success or gratification, which often leads to discouragement. They want what they want now, and if they don't get it now, they may even walk away and quit.

The one big difference between those who demonstrate the desire to stay the course and those who give up and go on to something else is patience. Lack of patience is one of the primary reasons why many athletes fail to enjoy solid skills development and growth. Patience's determining factor is what happens next.

When fully implementing skills growth with your athletic purpose, you must give those actions time to materialize. You don't get to the point of needing corrective action overnight, and effective change will not be evident for some time. Patience, Patience.

Are you numbered among those who are looking for coaches to give you three easy steps to success and then want these steps to create and engender enormously immediate progress? But meaningful skill modification takes time…and time takes patience.

So, when you are concerned about whether something will work, give it time. Giving any newly acquired skill or tactic a chance to improve your performance is best. Sit tight, be patient, and keep doing things to improve.

MONOTASKING

"Do one thing at once."

Let's take this theme of acquiring a new skill a step further. Do you exercise patience? What happens when you do not experience immediate success? Isn't there a tendency to forego the changes you have been working on after a few days, then gently slide right back into the old pattern?

Skills development occurs in stages. It takes time and effort to become a super athlete. Focus on improving a single skill and direct your efforts toward improving that single skill. This is what is known as monotasking.

Monotasking is the ability to embrace *"one thing at once."* The optimum for making positive changes is always focusing on improving one skill—or even one step in executing that skill—at a time. When you have mastered that step, it will spur you to master the next step.

Now, don't expect to develop a skill overnight fully. Research shows it takes about three weeks of conscious effort and hard work to do what needs to be done for the change to take hold. Then, you will need another month to get it firmly embedded in your mind and make it a significant part of your playing routine.

LEARN FROM EXAMPLE

> **Example is one of the greatest teachers for learning new and improving skills, techniques, methods, and tactics, provided, of course, that you are receptive to better ways of doing things.**

Are you thankful for the coaches and experienced players who show you how to perform the way you want to perform …who encourage you to improve and excel…who make you feel good about your ability? Attach yourself to a world of learning that benefits from the experience of others. These are the best resources available to you. Observe and listen to them with the intent of learning to improve.

We believe all successful athletes share a common thread: They seek out the experience of a coach, a mentor or someone to rely on to help them. Neither of us would be here talking about this without a coach who made a difference early in our athletic lives.

Who is the mentor in your athletic life who allows you to learn by example? As a regular learning source, how attentive are you to absorbing the great information laid out for you? It has to be continuous, for you don't know all you need to know about what you should know. In sports, more is caught than is taught.

Chapter Seven

A WILL TO PREPARE

> You must be willing to prepare at a level you have never prepared at before if you expect to perform at a level you have never performed at before. In essence, to experience something different, you have to be willing to prepare to do something different.

WILL TO PREPARE TO WIN

There is probably little difference between your athletic dreams and desires and those of almost any other athlete. All want to do well, achieve something significant, and be proud of themselves to have a substantial degree of success.

To put the finger on the one thing that makes a difference in most athletes' achievement level is the will to prepare to win. The willingness to prepare is the little difference that makes the big difference in converting dreams and desires into reality. Without question, the road to success is built on the will to prepare.

Coach Paul (Bear) Bryant said, *"The will to win matters... but in the scheme of winning, the will to prepare to win matters much more."* The most common cause of the lack of successful results is the absence of an aggressive will to win.

But the will to win will be a frustrated desire unless there is an ever-present will to prepare to win. The base of this preparation is built on what a better future would look, feel, and be like. It is doing things you have never consistently done before.

> Most athletes who have enjoyed tremendous success rarely were great in the beginning. But they were able to make themselves great because they knew they could be no better than the level of their preparation. They were aware they could only do what they were prepared to do. No more. No less.

"Prepare to do the things you are expected to do when you are expected to do them...so when it is time for the actual performance, you will do the things you are expected to in the way that you are expected to do them."
-Leonard Bernstein

"Highly successful athletes do not become successful doing things by the seat of their pants. They became successful through the long, lengthy hours of intense study, preparation and practice that helps make them successful."
-Bob Forsberg

> To become the athlete you want to be, you must understand why preparation is crucial. It means you have to undergo much trial and error. It would help if you worked hard to sharpen techniques, hone skills, and improve methods and tactics to reach a desirable performance level. It means you are always receptive to things that will help you perform better. Preparation connects you to a brighter future.

Nothing fails like success if it keeps you from learning new and better-performing habits. To have it the way you want it, you must move beyond the way it is.

Winning The "Head" Game

DEVELOPING PREPARATION HABITS

Everyone wants to be a winner until they understand what it takes to be a winner. Unmet expectations become the norm if knowledge, learning, and understanding lack the substance and direction to develop quality preparation habits.

Until there is an acceptance that preparation habits are crucial to success, how successful can any individual player or team be? Sitting back, hoping that a bit of action will be the magic pill leading to winning results, is the epitome of disappointment. To change reality, the perception of preparation must change.

Successful game results are triggered by a rush of deliberate and continuous action in the preparation phase of any sport. Listen to Coach Nick Saban: *"Winning is hard work and preparation. You can't be complacent...learn the process to success—what you are supposed to do and be able to go out there and do it consistently is the backbone of winning."*

Let us emphasize again that performing at your very best level every time you compete depends on your undertaking an intense and directed effort every time you train. Mechanics, techniques, and the like depend on going full blast at every training session. That's the best way to learn your assignments and how to execute them inside and out, up and down, backward and forward.

THOUGHTS ON PREPARATION

- Preparation may not always bring success, but there is no success without preparation.

- It is not preparing for the things you like to do that will make you more successful... It is preparing for the things you have to do to be successful.

- The fundamental theme behind all preparation efforts should be constantly moving beyond what you are for the greater achievement of what you can become.

- The goal of preparation is to help you know exactly what you are to do and to be confident in your abilities.

- A priceless performance at doing anything will always be preceded by paying the price at practice preparing for a priceless performance.

- Performing up to the very best level during every game opportunity is less a question of what you desire than what you are willing to do to prepare to perform at that level.

- The only way you can improve is to prepare in a way you have never prepared.

"You will never perform any better than your preparation habits allow you to perform."
-Paul (Bear) Bryant

IMPROVING PREPARATION HABITS

Two habits you must strive to eliminate...

- The habit of placing limits on yourself.
- The habit of letting others place limits on you.

The three stages of habits are:

- Stranger
- Companion
- Master (Good or Bad?)

A great way to improve your preparation habits is to:

- Seek the advice you need to have, not the advice you would like to hear.
- Be willing to attach yourself to those who know what you need to know.
- Ask questions…and listen to experienced voices that have been there and done what you want to do.

The big plays you make in a game are the little plays that you keep on improving in practice until they become a habit.

Winning The "Head" Game

If practice doesn't challenge you, it won't change you.

> If you keep doing what you have always done, you won't keep getting the results you have always gotten. That's because skills, methods, and tactics must be constantly upgraded to keep up with the changes happening around you...and within you.

A Matter of Habit

"My name is Habit. I am something that you created because of continual and similar behavior. I am your constant companion and closest friend.

Show me exactly how you want something done, and after a very short time, I will do it without your willful assent. It will become natural to me.

Most of your tasks will eventually become mine because I can do them without question or hesitation.

I am one of your greatest assets, provided you have trained me properly. But if you have not prepared me properly, my actions will rob you of the opportunity to do something different and better. Rest assured, that will be the case."

-Author unknown

"If you are not making some mistakes in practice, you are not working at it hard enough."
--Duffy Daugherty

"Practice only makes a difference when you practice the right kind of practice. To put it another way: Practice does not make perfect...perfect practice makes perfect."
-Vince Lombardi

"The successful teams do not become successful on the day of a game, they become successful on the long, lengthy hours on the practice field."
-Gene Stallings

"More games are won or lost on the parched soil of the practice field than they are on the green grass of the playing field."
-Weeb Eubanks

"The road to consistent winning run rights through the practice field."
-Vince Lombardi

"Practice works if everyone works at practice."
Dale Earnhardt

Daily Mental Practice Schedule

- Yesterday's performance will not affect today's effort.
- I will make my biggest practice goal today, one that out does yesterday.
- I will do something today at practice that will improve my performance at what I am expected to do.
- I will do everything expected of me today...and then some.
- I will perform today in such a way that tomorrow, I will be better.
- I will not concern myself with tomorrow's schedule today until today becomes tomorrow.

Chapter Eight

"SPREAD YOUR WINGS"

We believe virtually every young athlete will eventually want to experience something different—and better—in their play. To make this a reality, there must be a genuine commitment to doing something different. The energy to pursue something different with vigor and excitement lies within the consciousness of envisioning how that "something" will ultimately enrich performance. This is the first phase of any plan to improve your play.

The second phase is to develop a comprehensive strategy that lays out clear goals and objectives for being open to improvement. When your performance or actions are not generating the desired success, change is in order. The focus is on exploring methods and tactics to improve your overall performance.

Listen. Learn. Apply. The *"spread your wings"* concept involves concentrating on expanding your skill set and exploring ways to improve your effectiveness. Future growth is built around being flexible and mobile in the learning and development process.

The *"spread your wings"* questions before you are these: What are you willing to do differently to be more effective? Are you willing to step out of your comfort zone and expand your skills? Are you ready to explore new ways of performing and even venture into something unknown? Are you prepared to reach beyond, grasp the future, and do something that has not been a part of your routine?

The type and size of the changes you wish to make are based on what you and/or your coach(es) determine you need. The consequences of your choices will do one of two things: They will help clarify your commitments toward what you have been doing or lead you to make new decisions that will allow you to perform at a higher level.

The action phase is the last in the *"spread your wings"* equation. The difference-maker is to ensure that any adjustments you plan to make have you headed in the right direction. Redirection is only a plus if it is in the right direction. You may not always know for sure, but if you have done your homework, you know what changes are needed. Now, set up a preparation course that will enhance your effectiveness.

"Spreading your wings" works best when you make a sustained effort to focus on what will make you a better player. The utmost learning laboratory takes place during those hours you spend at practice working and digesting the things that will make you more effective. Engaging in repetitive action requires maximum attention and effort.

A given in sports—and life—is that if we do not expand, we are contracting. Life is lived on an incline. We either move forward or slide backward. If we are not expanding what we are, we are holding on to outdated, out-of-touch motives with the reality of an athletic world constantly moving forward.

Maximizing opportunities to improve your play is imperative to creating a more abundant and fulfilling future. The long-term benefits of establishing, maintaining, and improving your skillset and mental approach to the sport you play extend beyond what you can conceive in your present frame of mind.

However, you cannot attain this level of play if you hold onto and repeat inadequate habits from the past. This is where a lot of real work comes in.

It would help if you extended in the direction of where you have never been to change old habitual patterns and add new dimensions of habitual growth to your regular play. When you move toward expanding your playing habits, your capacity to change and adapt allows you to see possibilities that you have never seen before… possibilities that you had no idea existed.

"OPENNESS TO NEW EXPERIENCES"

There comes a time when you must push the reset button to advance. But the reset button carries an element of risk because it will involve doing things you have never done before.

Risk and opportunity tend to walk hand in hand along the road to progress. You must also seek the virtues of an *"openness to new experiences"* to keep you reaching and growing.

An *"openness to new experiences"* means comfortable habits do not imprison you. You are not trapped by routine. You do not cling to the familiar. You do not over-seek security nor choose the path of least resistance. You face the future with a staff in hand instead of a crutch.

Beethoven, the great music composer, had a favorite maxim: *"The barriers are not yet erected which can say to aspire talent and industry, 'thus far and no further.'"*

"Thus far and no farther" happens when you seek security at any cost, where there is no *"openness to experience."* You prefer to do things the same way, although that is not getting the job done.

RETROFITTING

There is no place where you suddenly become great at anything. Most overnight sensations take years to make a splash at what they do. They discovered that the route to top-notch performance is often slow and tedious.

This emphasizes truly understanding why steady improvement is crucial to enjoying future success. It means you have to undergo much trial and success. You must work hard to sharpen techniques, develop excellent skills, and improve attitudes to reach an acceptable performance level. It simply means you are always receptive to things that will enhance your play.

What you want to accomplish in sports starts with a comprehensive strategy called *retrofitting*. Retrofitting is a term used to describe how you need to continuously strive to improve.

The type and size of changes you make will either help clarify your commitments to your current actions or lead you to make more meaningful choices.

Quality athletic efforts depend on continual retrofitting. You cannot say there is nothing more to learn, no more skills to develop, no more challenges to be tackled, and no more new tactics and techniques to try. It would help if you never feared making appropriate changes in your performance.

A retrofitting mentality helps you adjust to the changes happening around you. It keeps you on your toes, actively seeking out beneficial adjustments in your performance. Retrofitting is at the core of your ability to move beyond the old ways of doing things when they can no longer guarantee high productivity.

Regardless of the sport, they each present a persistent learning laboratory by repeating the same lessons until they are learned. So, analyze, evaluate, and keep practicing. That is what will improve your game on an ongoing basis.

Retrofitting involves seeking new avenues for improving one's performance base. A significant part of this responsibility is having a "now" attitude. Retrofitting doesn't start tomorrow or the next day, but now. It is ongoing or non-going.

One final thought about retrofitting. It may mean you must delve into the unknown…into trying something new and different. You are probably not going to feel comfortable with it at first. But hang with it, you will get a handle on it soon. Count on it.

> **If you keep doing what you have always done, you won't keep getting the results you have always gotten. That's because skills, methods, and tactics must be constantly upgraded to keep up with the changes happening around you…and within you.**

Chapter Nine

PLAY TO WIN

Athletes are limited by their talents, abilities, and resources in the extent to which they can satisfy their dreams and desires. However, the most influential limit is not what they are but rather what they decide to do with what they are. The course athletes follow in taking what they have and making it better is influenced by how they move on beyond any fears that hold them back.

A high level of success requires a high level of risk. If you let fear limit your ability to take the necessary risk, you may reduce your expectations and shift to a lower gear. To succeed extraordinarily, calculated risks must be taken particularly.

Has taking risks been a challenge for you? If it has been, sense yourself reaching beyond the status quo to grasp the new and different. Visualize stretching yourself and extending your capabilities. See yourself doing the things you never imagined you could do. You are now ready to experience results that you have never experienced before.

Store these words of Darwin P. Kingsley away somewhere in your mental computer:

> *"There are no limitations in what you can do except the limitations in your own mind as to what you cannot do."*

JUST DO IT

- To do what you always have done won't get what you have always gotten.

- Do what you have never done to enjoy what you have never had.
- Do things you dislike to experience things you do like.
- To experience something different, you must be willing to do something different.

> **Top athletes have built their success around the attitude of "I'll DO, not I'll TRY." They do their very best right where they are, just as they are. They have learned that having a DOING attitude enhances the odds of creating winning opportunities.**

Self-Confidence

Sometimes, the most challenging part of the journey is accepting the fact you are worthy of the trip.

You are limited in how much your talents, abilities, and resources can satisfy your dreams and desires. However, the most influential limit is not what you are but what you decide to do with what you are. The course you follow in taking what you have and improving it is influenced by your self-confidence level and the risks you are willing to take. To succeed, one must possess incredible self-confidence.

Many talented athletes fail to measure up to their potential because of their lack of self-confidence. Significant factors interfering with self-confidence are low self-esteem, fundamental insecurity, an inferiority complex, or simple overall self-doubt.

Often, at the base of this self-doubt, we are told early in life that we are not good enough or incapable of succeeding in athletics, or anything else. Is this a challenge for you? Don't you dare, for one more second, believe the comments of others unaware of your potential for greatness. You have got what it takes. Believe it with all your heart.

Winning The "Head" Game

Most of the time, these comments come from those close to you because they don't want to see you get hurt if you fail. We both understand this very well. We overcame significant negativism around us to move on with our careers and lives.

Let us emphasize again that building a bright future depends on possessing self-confidence par excellence. Your remarkable capabilities will grow as your self-confidence grows. Conquer this self-confidence quest to set the stage for fulfilling your potential as an athlete. It is no secret that how you view yourself will play a crucial role in your future.

Chapter Four highlights how self-talk makes a big difference in raising your self-image and self-confidence. If you tend to look at the "negatives" about yourself at the expense of your many "positive" qualities, the points below should be of great interest to you in building your self-confidence:

Be prepared. Knowledge management is crucial to developing self-confidence. The more you know, the more comfortable you feel in performing what you know. The reality is you will ultimately do what you are prepared to do.

Develop a growth mindset. A great way to get out of a self-deprecating and low self-esteem loop is to think about where you are headed, not where you have been. Focus on what you will do to make progress today

Be excited about what you do. Being fired up about tackling the tasks and challenges you face is a vital step to building self-confidence. They give you a chance to get better.

Stay active. You cannot acquire self-confidence sitting around waiting for something to happen. It would be best if you were actively involved in developing skills, improving overall abilities, and expanding your confidence level.

Speak the winners' language. We covered this earlier. It is so important. Talk to yourself like a winner. The positive affirmations you tell yourself are vital to self-confidence and longevity. Be a self-coach, not a self-critic.

Conduct mental rehearsals. Visualize in your mind's eye what you will do today to make positive things happen. The results can dramatically enhance self-confidence when you conduct mental trials and follow with responsive action.

Expect the best. When you participate mentally in the conviction that something good will happen today, that is the direction your confidence level will take.

Exercise patience. A deep and abiding confidence in yourself is something that takes time. It must be coaxed step by step. In the end, what you earn will be the result of short, consistent gains.

Act the part. Act the role until you feel comfortable playing the role. Be a beacon of confidence around others. Nothing is more enlightening to others than letting your light shine so brightly that they will want to do the same.

Associate with winners. Spend little time with those who are a haven for negative thoughts. You gain self-confidence by associating with those who encourage you…who see you as being worthy of tackling your most formidable challenge…who appreciate that you have what it takes to make it big in the world of athletics.

Celebrate your successes. Celebrate every victory, no matter how small or insignificant it may seem. Giving yourself a pat on the back occasionally is okay—if you do something worthy, express your appreciation- but don't rest on your laurels. Use your successes to build on to develop the confidence to stretch out toward future success.

Don't wait until everything is just right before you act. It will never be perfect. There will always be challenges, obstacles, roadblocks, and less-than-ideal conditions.

> **Challenges are always present. Keep on going. With each step you take, you will grow stronger and stronger, more skilled, more self-confident, and more successful. That's the right direction.**

The more challenges you face, the more chances you have to be successful. And from it comes the supportive feeling that you threw your hat in the ring and tried to make something positive happen. Around the winners' circle that attitude counts for something very special.

> **Do what you must do when you must do it, and you will have a good chance of having what you want when you want to have it.**

"PLAYING TO WIN"

Years ago, I (Lou) was sitting in Coach Bum Phillips's office the day after his heavy underdog New Orleans Saints football team had upset the Los Angeles Rams. He was speaking with a sports reporter and said something I have never forgotten: *"We were playing to win while they were playing to keep from losing."*

The more I thought about that statement, the more I realized how true it was. Several questions arise from Bum's quote that we should ask ourselves: What kind of frame of mind do we possess when approaching a difficult task or a crucial situation? Do we focus on what can go right? Or is our attention geared primarily to what might go wrong? Good questions.

When your attention is centered around what can go right and your actions reflect this positive approach, the odds will be in your favor for success. You can make great things happen by focusing on what you should do to succeed.

Conversely, when you consistently think about what you shouldn't do where is the accent being placed? What are you focusing on? Aren't you intuitively tuning into the negatives, not the positives? We have said that before…and we probably will again.

To avoid a negative "*keep from losing*" attitude, you must refrain from thinking about the negatives that can hold you back. Emphasizing the positive—which makes up a success-oriented attitude—will most likely direct your performances in a way that makes your intended outcome a reality.

Which is more indicative of you? Is this an area in your mindset that you need to take a serious look at?

Occasionally, it is essential to check your focus. Ask yourself: *"Am I focusing on what I can do rather than what I cannot do? Am I focusing on what can go right, rather than on what might go wrong? Am I focusing on what it takes to be successful, or am I focusing on what it takes to keep from failing? Am I focusing on playing to win or keep from losing?"*

NOT LOSING

I (Sonny) believe winning is important, but not losing may be more critical. Think about that for a minute. You see, losing engenders negative feelings and consequences, and given enough time and pressure, it leads to a general downward spiral for a team. In some situations, it often leads to the same within a community. For better or worse, sports have become that important in communities nationwide.

My feeling is that the priority is to find ways to avoid losing. You will find this quote elsewhere: *"The best thing that should come from losing is the feeling you don't like it."* A team with that attitude permeates has taken a step toward finding ways to avoid losing.

Developing a winning culture is no easy task. Winning is by design, not by accident. The road to winning (and losing, for that matter) is always under construction. They recognize that the architect of a winning culture will produce a very different route to travel. That route begins with concentrating on a positive environment of words and actions.

This book has focused on that. The insight in these pages sustains and further reflects upon the continuous flow of positive-building activity, which portrays winning as a destination and a journey. In that regard, every moment, every minute, every hour, every day a coach or player is involved in an athletic endeavor, the focus is on developing or sustaining a winning culture.

Pay attention to everything that is happening now with consciously heightened awareness. A winning culture may not come immediately. It may only look like a good idea. But there is an opportunity—there is possibility—if you focus on the here and now.

That's right. The key factor is to realize that winning is encoded in the here and now. It is always now that you should be thinking about doing what it takes to be a winner—not earlier, not later, not yesterday, not tomorrow, but right now. Center your attention on fully and completely investing this moment, focusing on winning thoughts as if it were your only moment. Winning is a consequence of a now thing. In the present, you build a more favorable foundation going forward.

> **You know what you have done. You know how far you have come. But if you don't know what you can do, you don't know how far you can go. The challenge before you every day is to keep expanding your horizons as if there are no limits to your potential. It is a challenge you can meet when you always strive to make prudent decisions today that will impact tomorrow.**

A LITTLE BIT MORE

Four short words sum up what lifts most successful athletes above the crowd:

-A LITTLE BIT MORE-

They do all that is expected of
them, and then -- *a little bit more.*

Do you really want to step out of the crowd and be something special? Develop the habit of doing something extra by subscribing to the mentality of doing *"A Little Bit More."* If you see something that needs to be done, do you wait to be told before doing it? Or do you take the initiative and get on with it, even if there may be no personal gain for you?

Successful people think about how to do things better, not a great deal better, just a little bit better. They turn their attention not only to what needs to be done but instinctively to what is yet to be done. They don't sit back and wait for something to come along to do…they go out and make something happen. They are always working to improve every day.

"A little bit more" attitude pays off in many ways. One of the most prominent is it helps everyone around you feel better about you. It enhances your standing with your colleagues, coaches, and others close to you.

"A little bit more" attitude can give you a big edge in sport(s) you play. If you want to get ahead, take advantage of those in charge by doing more than they asked you to do, and keep on doing it!

DO SOMETHING SPECIAL

- Give the team a sample of the best you--and do something special.
- Use your body, mind, and God-given talents--and do something special.
- Take instructions well, apply what you learn with all your might, and do something special.
- Let the role you play on the team be more significant and finer than a heartbeat--and do something special.

- Play your role to the best of your ability every time you participate--and you will do something special.

> **Winners visualize opportunities for big success and they take them. They appreciate that if they are going to miss, they make it a big miss.**

MAJOR IN MINORS

There is very little difference between being good and being great in sports. Being great is not necessarily made up of doing the big things -- even though they are essential. The real difference in attaining greatness is measured by how enthusiastically you stretch out to perform the little things that other less successful athletes would not consider worth doing. Never underestimate the role of minor things.

Being a champion athlete is nothing more than many little things done well. Make no mistake: you must learn how to do the little things before you can do the big things that will make you big.

Everyday attention to little things is no little thing. When you make the most of the little ones, big opportunities tend to come. Progress is built on doing the little things you haven't done.

You will only be as big as the little things that are generally important. So, never feel too big to do the little things that have a way of leading you to enjoy the big and best things in life. Here are some additional suggestions:

- Everyday attention to little things is no little thing.
- You will only be as big as the little things, which will help you focus on the critical things.
- Champions do the little things without being told to do them… and keep doing them.
- Luck is by design. The evolutionary nature of luck is that the better you do little things, the luckier you become.

HUSTLE IS

HUSTLE IS an indirect yet decisive daily movement toward the pursuit of an upward path.

HUSTLE IS elbow grease, pushing and pulling, and effort.

HUSTLE IS doing all that is expected of you–even if no coach is watching.

HUSTLE IS staying the course through grit and grime... sweat and tears... bumps and bruises.

HUSTLE IS having a strong work ethic to get a handle on any challenge, and then tackling it with the best of your ability.

HUSTLE IS doing your best with conditions as you find them -- even if you would like to have a different set of conditions.

HUSTLE IS continuing to do something that all around you are certain cannot be done.

HUSTLE IS doing the little things others would not think worth doing... and doing them well.

HUSTLE IS going hard enough on your first wind to see if you have a second.

HUSTLE IS working hard to maximize your strengths and minimize your weaknesses.

HUSTLE IS doing the things you have to do -- when you must do them -- to make positive things happen.

HUSTLE IS the condition created when you get desire and enthusiasm moving in the same direction.

HUSTLE IS racing to fulfill a dream with no speed limit on the pursuit of excellence and generation of success.

HUSTLE IS in the words of the great coach, Vince Lombardi, "...that moment when you have worked your heart out and lie exhausted on the field of battle -- victorious."

Chapter Ten

WINNING TRAITS

We wanted to present what we believe are thirteen (13) non-negotiable traits for your review. Athletes who enthusiastically embrace the traits (in alphabetical order) of Adaptability, Anticipation, Attentive Presence, Commitment, Competitiveness, Consistency, Effort, Integrity, Mental Toughness, Now Courage, Passion, Pressure Tolerance, and Self-discipline are on a course toward enjoying higher possibilities in their athletic careers.

ADAPTABILITY

Sports are characterized by sudden, unexpected, and sometimes dramatic challenges. The capacity to rise effectively to meet these challenges is crucial for almost any athlete. A knack for adopting a decide-to-decide attitude can often make the slightest difference in producing significant results.

Functioning in a rapidly changing environment requires developing a flexible, malleable ability to adapt. An adaptive mindset is a conditioned mind that has been systematically trained, focused, concentrated, and tempered to reconcile and cope with the immediate external changes in sports. Adaptive thinking helps you apply sound reasoning in recognizing and perceiving the actual reality of sports action quickly and more correctly.

Armed with adaptability, you can maintain composure even in the most competitive and pressure-filled situations. It is through an adaptive mindset you learn to avoid extremes and overreactions. Adapting quickly and efficiently minimizes the emotional surges during actual game action and gives you a stable power source.

Adaptability is a learned behavior. It is essential to your ability to make sound and practical adjustments in your skill set. Realizing that game situation variations can challenge your ability to cope calls for adaptability in your core skills.

Letting go is never easy. Altering how you have done things requires the highest level of adaptive behavior. The quicker you can get into a groove, the more flexibility you display when participating in an actual game.

Sometimes, the "old ways" are the only ways because that's what you first learned. But if your primary skills need refining, you must be ready to "let go" to create room for something better. One of the most challenging things to do is to detach yourself from those things that make you feel "comfortable" and expand your experience and knowledge base.

How you approach changing your "old ways" makes all the difference in whether you are successful. We are discussing creating an adaptive mindset where things improve because you have the fortitude and drive to discover how to improve them. This mindset leads to a deep commitment to adapt.

A simple fact when the intent is to adapt to new and more constructive ways of doing things is that you never let go entirely of the past. There will always be something of the past left within you. Every new beginning carries with it a lesson from things you have done. There is always something from the past that can be adaptive to the future.

Do you believe there is something better out there than you have ever experienced? If the answer is "Yes," then your ability to adapt and do something different must be done deliberately.

Adaptability works best when you are proactive from the insight that enables you to be reactive to needed adjustments. Armed with this kind of foresight, you can develop an arsenal of diverse playing strategies and tactics that will help you unlock the door to future athletic growth and development.

Winning The "Head" Game

ANTICIPATION

The most significant way to become a better performer during a game is to be the creator of the action, not its effect. This begins with being more mindful of the three things needed to maximize your play: perception of the action, processing the action and performing based on the action. Being highly effective in these three areas depends on maximizing your ability to anticipate.

Success in most sports is often measured in fractions of seconds. The ability to react quickly and effectively accelerates the decision-making process, giving you an edge in competitive situations. Anticipating what might happen improves reaction time…something crucial in sports of any kind.

Reaction time is simply the brief interval between initiating the game or match action and determining how to react to that action. The one constant here is that a delay in anticipation, regardless of the situation, can affect reaction time. For example, a football linebacker is a fraction of a second late in reacting to a play and misses a tackle, which results in a big yardage gain.

What is the key to maximizing reaction time? Some athletes may have more innate response skills than others, but others can improve their reaction time by developing anticipatory skills.

Quality anticipation requires attentive presence in the present moment. A constant and deepening moment-by-moment mindfulness during the game action will lead to more appropriate and quicker responses.

The lack of complete focus and concentration adversely affects anticipation and reaction time. But when you more openly anticipate what may happen before it happens, you maximize reaction time.

The ideal way to become more anticipatory is to possess a more present-tense mindset. You can train yourself to think only of the here and now. Consciously think about how to keep your attention on the task at hand. The more you focus on the present, the more alert you are reacting to what happens now.

Whatever you are doing, focus on what possibilities may arise. Raise your attention and energy to the highest level possible every moment you are involved in the action. This will enhance your consciousness and elevate your level of play. You will actually notice things you have not been thoughtful of before. Never underestimate the importance of anticipation.

ATTENTIVE PRESENCE

Attention leads to intentions.

Why is it difficult to be fully attentive to anything? The world is full of distractions, lessening the ability to provide undivided attention. Getting to know a potential customer is directly proportional to diligently *"being in their presence with your total being."* Block out the distractions and provide a willing ear.

Elsewhere in the book, we discuss monotasking. It is said that the quickest way to get many things done is to do only one thing at once. The vital truth is that directing all your attention and energy toward the action enables a more excellent perception. Being capable and thorough in assessing the action leads to reacting to what is going on more rapidly.

Learning to concentrate on each play as it occurs is an acquired trait. It is impossible to force yourself to focus on anything! The ability to concentrate is formulated around the habit of being overly interested in a specific thing. Focus naturally happens when you desire to actively engage as much as possible in the action occurring at any moment.

Again, let us emphasize that the key to *"being wherever you are"* prominently depends on blocking the distracting things happening around you and within you. Focus on one thing—or one person—at a time, and prioritize that.

The more you apply the *"focus on one thing at a time"* theme, the greater your anticipatory action will be. When your concentration is intense, you refrain from ever considering the possibility that you may not anticipate the action.

Winning The "Head" Game

Try these thoughts on focusing on:

- It is worth remembering that whatever gets your attention gets you.... for wherever your real focus is, that's where your heart will be.

- When you absorb yourself in the action, a setback will not fracture your approach—forit will only be temporary.

- Focus on each situation as it appears. You cannot do everything that needs to be done at once... but you can do the one thing that needs to be done at once.

- When you focus on the task, you are less sensitive to the "negatives" around you—the things that work against you. Make the effort to take a positive approach toward what you are working on at any time.

- Your best chance is where you are right now... for what you might be "no chance" may well be your only chance.

- When you are "always where you are"—you will always be **focused** on something that will move you forward.

- Always concentrate on your role -- not what others do or are supposed to do—and initiate the effort to perform your role to the best of your ability.

- *"Those who lose focus -- lose."* The vital truth is that you will never perform quite as capably as possible unless you direct all your energy toward one situation or task.

"Wherever you are, be there."

COMMITMENT: THE SOUL OF WINNERS

The quality of your athletic experience will be directly proportional to your commitment to being a top-notch athlete. Commitment is about choices, not conditions. Commitment helps you fight any impediments that could keep you from any goal.

Nothing great is ever accomplished without commitment to the process that has been proven to be successful. Commitment is the common denominator among those who become consistent winners. It requires a heart and soul effort–and you can only put your heart and soul in it when committed with your whole being.

Commitment is about choosing to believe that something can be done better. It is about choosing to believe that you can succeed. The more committed you are to accomplishing something, the more likely you will find a way to make it a reality. Being inspired by a commitment to succeed makes challenging situations appear less complicated and more doable.

The source of commitment arises deep within your very being. Innate talent isn't what will place you among the best; instead, it is simply your commitment to maximizing your talent. To say it another way, *"Your skills and abilities won't get you up in the morning, but your commitment to be a top athlete will."*

If you are committed, you are driven by something deeper than interest. Being driven is a gut reaction to an intense internal craving. It works its way down through the creases and grooves to settle quietly into the corners of your whole being.

How committed are you to becoming a superb athlete? Get the commitment factor right—first. Once it is solidified, it becomes the core of your passion for being something special.

Commitment centers around a WILL-DO attitude, for when WILL DO shows up—HOW TO is not far behind.

COMPETITIVENESS

We have seen numerous athletes who had a chance to be great but lacked the competitiveness necessary to put them over the top. The ability to be competitive is a team core value that cannot be any more personal. Believe us, the higher you expect to go in any sport, the more competitive you must become. The reason is simple enough: the higher up the success ladder you hope to climb, the more formidable the competition you will face.

Winning The "Head" Game

Possessing a strong desire to be the best at the role chosen for you to play is the centerpiece of competitiveness. But you must apply common sense and not let your competitiveness override your better judgment in your drive to be the best. Just possess balance in your endeavor to be more successful as a competitor.

Digest these great words on the reality of the competition:

- The size of the competition is about the same as your overall attitude toward the competition.
- The competition is competing against you--not you against the competition.
- If you become afraid that the competition is better than you are, at some point, the competition will be.
- The key to enhancing your competitiveness is to focus on what you can do, not on what the competition may or may not be able to do.
- It is hard sometimes to live with tough competition, but it is harder to live without them. They motivate you to work harder--and smarter.
- Never underestimate the capabilities of any competitor. The lost column is full of those teams who have taken their competitors lightly.
- Good competitors provide a clearer picture of what you must do to improve. They give you a real sense of your level of competitiveness and what to do to improve
- Overcoming the challenges of the competition is the only way to develop and build a future—quality competitors produce the soil in which you will do your best growing.
- If it were not for the stiff competition that you face, what would you do with yourself? Be thankful for the strong competition you encounter. It gives you a chance to see just how good you can be.
- When you have something to prove, there is nothing better than a competitive situation to prove it.

- A competitive situation is a natural habitat for a winner. Winners study their competitors' strengths and weaknesses, tendencies and tactics... and game plans. Winners know their competition and are mentally ready.

"Your teammates ordinarily test you at practice, but the real test is provided by your game day or match opponents. So, from this standpoint, you can consider your opponents to be great teachers, and you need to be thankful they give you the chance to learn how to get better."
-John McEnroe

CONSISTENCY

This is one of the most essential traits of an athlete. To reach a high level, you have to execute your responsibilities and assign tasks with a high level of consistency. A necessary aspect of attaining this consistency is translating from practice to game situations with an elevated execution level. The expectation is always to strive to perform a little better each game.

Top athletic status is neither magical nor mysterious. It is the natural consequence of consistently applying fundamentals. Whatever you want to achieve in sports will not come without consistency in the basics. Consistency is essential.

It is essential to recognize that enjoying a higher success level in sports represents a feat just as substantial as getting to that level in the first place. It takes a consistent and determined daily training effort always to perform your best.

Consistency is behind the belief that you will always come through... execute to the best of your ability and strive to do the things you must do when you must do them. It truly believes that every opportunity counts for building a brighter future. Consistency rises out of the feeling that you must give your best every time to receive the best. The height of your achievements will be solidified in direct proportion to the level of your consistency.

Winning The "Head" Game

EFFORT

Why do two people with comparable abilities and skill sets end up worlds apart in results? Even a person with only average ability and skills may consistently perform above the level of their requirements, while another person with exceptional ability regularly fails to enjoy quality results.

A significant part of the answer to this question can be found in their work ethic. Work ethics determine how much effort one puts into turning dreams into reality. It is a core value based on solid effort, durable work, and impeccable diligence. Those with strong, positive work habits tend to get a leg up on others because they work efficiently and wiser.

Effort is an inherent attitude that a person develops about themselves and the quality and depth of their work ethic. Those individuals with inadequate effort tend to do just enough to get by and will probably eventually see their dreams go up in smoke. Quality application in everything you do can become part of your belief system. That's a philosophy that will carry you a long way.

What is your philosophy of effort? Do you possess a soaring level of intensity in your work patterns? This is the one thing that is definitely in your own hands. You have complete control over it. Focusing and developing the best work habits you can muster leads to more positive outcomes and superb overall results.

Those with solid effort are intrinsically motivated to do their best and are rewarded by delivering consistently high results. Through sheer willpower and determination, they value doing what is expected of them to the best of their ability. Then, as we discussed earlier, they do a little more. They go beyond what is expected and are even required to solve problems and seek new opportunities above their typical responsibilities.

The ladder to sports success is built on the effort you put into your adventure—and how it is cultivated through daily use. Someone aptly pointed out: *"Hard work beats talent when talent doesn't work hard."* Take that to heart.

It is crucial to your future to understand that performing well can never be regarded as incidental or accidental. It is a direct reflection of your attitude toward employing quality work ethics. Drawing on the solid effort that you use will help you to develop and grow your business continually.

The experience of quality effort leads to getting more done in less time. This creates more growth opportunities. Buried deep in applying yourself with a strong work ethic is how it speeds up getting to the "good part" faster. Applying yourself in a bigger and broader way will get more done. An intense effort may be your number one asset in the larger scheme of things.

__Effort arises from both physical capacity and a steadfast and determined effort to succeed.__

INTEGRITY

__Integrity is the basis for respect, dignity, and trust… it is choosing value over any aspect of personal gain.__

Integrity demonstrates that you always function within the confines of a societal and personal code of morality, establishing you as a just and right person. Integrity cannot be forged, nor can one borrow, buy, or steal it. Like the markings ingrained in the very heart of a tree, integrity is made palpable by what's on the inside. Integrity functions inside out.

Integrity is earned by consistently proving through words and actions that upholding a moral standard is a higher priority than what can be gained without it. It cannot be achieved in sporadic acts of doing the right thing to satisfy the conscious at any moment. It is doing what is ethically correct all the time, regardless of being noticed or acknowledged by others.

If unchecked, undisciplined ambition can lead to highly unethical practices. To attain a higher level of people skills success, an effective compromise must be found, but not to the point of prohibitive cost. The secret is to strive for balance and ensure integrity is left intact and not used as a bargaining tool.

Winning The "Head" Game

When conscious movement is away from things in sports—and life—those lower internal values, the natural movement is toward higher-level values. Every day, situations are met, creating challenges to right or wrong, good or bad, just or unjust decisions. Most of these situations are routine, but some are unique, while others are important. Almost every choice made and every action taken in these situations has integrity at its core.

One of the most demanding forms of mental toughness is deciding what you can live with tomorrow, not what you might get away with today. This requires constantly calibrating a mindset that continually and consistently maintains the fiber of integrity.

The marvel of integrity is that it can be developed and nurtured. It begins with having a clear picture of the quality of the athlete you want to be and then acting according to that image without exception. It takes a focused and disciplined approach.

What is the number one thing to bring to the team? It is the best *you*. People want to be involved with someone who is authentic and exudes confidence. You are a person of integrity. You feel good about yourself. The infinite truth of what you are is evident.

Make everyone associated with the team excited that you are a part of the team. So, spend time doing things that enrich your value for yourself and improve your value for others. That's a great place to be.

MENTAL TOUGHNESS

"When the going gets tough, the tough are already going."
"Where there's a will there is a way."
"Never, never give in."

Heard any of these before? If you have been around the sports world for any length of time, we guarantee you have. Without a doubt, these statements are factual. Tenacious people tend to win.

The question here concerns something other than physical toughness, which is earned through preparation, practice, and hard work. The answer concerns the development of mental toughness.

There is no light switch to flip to turn on your mental toughness. Physicality helps, but mental toughness is rooted deeper in yourself. It is very personal. It is more of a heart thing than a mind thing.

One of the givens of athletics is that circumstances can change on a dime. Challenges pop up regularly. Without the challenges you face, the pitfalls you encounter, and the obstacles you overcome, how do you find out just how good you can be?

A shortcoming in developing mental toughness is the inability to recognize and appreciate that obstacles and difficulties are the only way to grow in personal responsibility. There is no sport where you can achieve significant success without encountering and overcoming adverse or challenging situations.

The elements of success are found in your ability to develop mental toughness that is readily available when those demanding situations arise. That might require a shift in habits. It might require that you rewire and retool the way you think. You may even need to see differently. But you are up for it, aren't you?

The gift of mental toughness is that there is no reasonable obstacle you cannot overcome and stay on course to achieve a goal. In essence, you see opportunity where others see dangerous obstacles in your path. Does that sounds like you?

> ***Toughness is in your soul and***
> ***spirit, not in your muscles.***

NOW COURAGE

The opposite of fear is said to be courage. Fear is a mindset. Courage is an action. Courage works from the inside out. It changes how you think... speak... and act. But it is only worthy when applied "now," where it is most needed.

Moving beyond what you are and stretching out toward what you want to be as an athlete requires action. Action requires employing the traditional trait of courage–or, as we prefer, courage *now*. Courage is the ability to initiate a solitary act of doing something to improve your level of play—and doing it now.

The power of *now* courage is well documented. The fundamental forces that worked eons before still work now. But courage is not an all-encompassing trait. It may be present in one situation but not in another, which is quite common for most of us.

The challenge of *now* courage is the inability to see what is on the other side. You probably have some idea of what is expected when you arrive there. But if you are not careful, you will conjure up "negatives" about what's ahead. Let *now* courage lead the way.

The same *now* courage that got you headed in the right direction is the same *now* courage that will give you a deep belief in the amazing opportunities that exist in your future.

One of the most therapeutic things you can do to establish the *now* courage that will move you beyond any fear is the power of suggestion. You may never know how to function without chaos until you make the mental suggestion to use your faith in yourself to move you beyond any fear.

It is not hard to act when you must…the key is having the now courage to act when nothing is pushing you.

PASSION

There is a significant difference between being interested in something and being passionate about making it a part of your life. When you are interested in something, you work at it only when convenient. When you are passionate about something, you do it with all your being.

Your goal should be to become something special in whatever sport(s) you play and your role in that sport(s). To reach this worthy goal, your desire to become significantly good at any sport should make passion a significant part of your strategy. Be willing to dig passionately deep and discover how to become the athlete you want to be.

Your passion for doing and becoming your best will always serve you well. This passion sparks the desire to be locked into doing what is necessary to grow beyond the performance levels that far exceed your original expectations.

Your passionate desire is nurtured from the inside out. It originates in a heart that yearns to ride the winds of successful adventure. It is the key to developing who you are to become. Others may not remember your exact actions, but they will remember the passion you demonstrated in your actions. Is your PASS-I-ON worth passing on?

- Establishing a deep-felt passion for what you are doing is at the heart of commitment. This passion sparks the commitment to do your best.
- Passion keeps you going and growing. Through passion, you answer the question: *"How can I do better?"*
- You must be willing to give of yourself to receive something passionately…and passion comes first.
- Passion is nurtured from the inside out. It originates in a heart that yearns to ride the winds of adventure. It is the key to beginning the process of greatness.
- Others may not remember your exact actions, but they will remember the passion you demonstrated in your actions. Is your PASS-I-ON worth passing on?

"A vision for the future arises from your passion…not your position."
-Dr. John Maxwell

PRESSURE TOLERANCE

When right on the brink of making a key decision or executing a play in a crucial game situation, some athletes flinch… retreat…, or lose courage at the very moment it is most needed. Why? Our experience is that the perception of a critical point in a game is inherently altered by one of the most notable opiates known to athletes: *pressure*.

Winning The "Head" Game

How good are you at handling so-called *"pressure situations?"* How do you react amid stressful circumstances? Does your heart begin to pound more than usual? Do your palms become sweaty? Does a big lump develop in your throat? Do you doubt whether you can meet the stressful situation head-on and create the desired outcome? Experienced athletes who can handle crucial game conditions that have been labeled as *"pressure situations"* are the ones who have a leg up on attaining quality status.

A truism of "pressure situations" is that they can either bring out the best in you–or the worst—depending on how you view and handle the situation. When released inwardly, pressure can negatively impact performance by producing distinct physiological changes in the body.

When turned inward, the stress created in *"pressure situations"* limits reaction time. Blood vessels constrict, reducing the blood supply to the brain and affecting the ability to think clearly. The results are predictable: how you perform is less than what it is under different circumstances.

There is a brighter side to the stress produced by pressure...it doesn't always have to be negative. It can be a real positive force. Those so-called "pressure situations" can bring greater depth and meaning to your play. This may vary from task to task...from game situation to game situation, depending on what you are facing. But we assure you that you can translate the pressurized moments in sports by internalizing the following important lessons:

- The season's first contest is just as important as the last.
- One game is never more critical than another game.
- One play is never more critical than another play.
- Focus on what you have been trained to do in every play, in every situation; then, no one situation is ever more critical than the next--they are all critical.
- There are no pressure situations...only situations where participants feel or experience pressure.

The word *pressure* is tossed around and is a natural part of the sports vernacular. However, those so-called *"pressure situations"* you encounter carry the same weight as any other situation.

The secret to making the best of those pressure situations is to embrace where you are and visualize performing optimally what you are expected to do. **The focus is on the "how to" and not the results**. This is the best way for those so-called "pressure situations" to have minimal control over your actions. It simply depends on how you manage it through exercising pressure tolerance.

SELF-DISCIPLINE

The depths of your self-discipline will gauge the height of your athletic success. It is the foundation on which you will turn your talents into quality abilities.

When you are told you need to be more disciplined, what does that mean to you? We would venture to say that for athletic purposes, discipline is the bridge between the role you are asked to play and your ability to keep your focus on playing that role. We believe that discipline holds the key to the innate ability to focus on executing the task you are performing--not on what the result of the execution might mean. This route generally leads to a much more satisfying conclusion.

Executing a task is more powerful when you have a built-in ability to focus specifically on a task. In other words, a steady, disciplined approach will always exceed a wavering one.

What mental discipline do you possess when approaching a difficult or crucial task? Do you focus on what can go right? Or is your attention geared predominantly to what might go wrong?

When you discipline yourself to only think about the things you should be doing, the things that can go right, your actions will reflect this positive approach. The odds will be in your favor for success when you keep your eyes on what you should be doing to execute the role you have been trained to perform successfully.

Conversely, when you consistently think about what you shouldn't do rather than what you should do, where is your effort being placed? Aren't you intuitively tuning in to the "don'ts instead of the "dos" -- the negatives instead of the positives?

To avoid a negative "keep from failing" attitude, you must discipline yourself to refrain from thinking about the negatives that can hold you back. A disciplined approach that emphasizes the positive—what you can do—will most likely direct your performances in a way that makes your intended outcome a successful reality.

Which is more indicative of you? Is this an area in your mindset toolbox that you need to take a serious look at? Occasionally, it is essential to check your focus. Ask yourself questions like: *"Am I disciplined enough to focus on what I can do rather than what I cannot do? Am I disciplined enough to focus on what can go right rather than on what might go wrong? Am I disciplined enough to focus on what it takes to succeed, focused on what it takes to keep from failing?"*

A SONNY MOMENT

Every good player has their mind wrapped around most of the winning traits mentioned in this chapter, at least to a favorable degree. These great traits lie right at the core of a winning mindset.

A winning player has a specific look. I know it when I see it, but it is not easy to describe. I will give it a go and provide my thoughts on what creates a quality player.

There are generally only a few top-notch players on a team. While these are more excellent performers than most other players, they are not better than anyone else. Think about that for a minute. The play of the top players on a team is a step above the play of others, but the best players know that without the quality efforts of their teammates, their role has been futile.

The top players have propelled themselves to embrace the rare luxury of excellence. They are a model of consistency. As someone so appropriately said, *"Top performers produce a symphony of coordinated motions, which renders their performance virtually fluid and almost effortlessly."*

Over the years, I had many good players who overcame significant deficits and disadvantages in talent and abilities. Through an intense work ethic and determination, they emerged as quality athletes. Others sustained a discouraging injury and had to struggle through rehabilitation. Because of these experiences, they had to call on many difference-making attributes to mentally prepare themselves for putting in the time and effort to rise above the challenges they had faced. They acquired the ability to grasp and utilize the winning traits described in this chapter.

I want to say something about the difference-makers I saw among these players. First, they possessed an even temperament. They not only learned how to play at a higher level, but they also learned how to conduct themselves on a higher plane. They had an emotional handle on the tension and mental anguish that arose during competitive events.

These players demonstrated a significant in-game presence, significantly impacting the team's performance. The ultimate test of being a winning player is the ability to make a mark upon game action in such a way as to alter the direction of the action. That's what elevates the top players to extraordinary heights. But even if the top players exhibit Herculean efforts, it still rests with their teammates to work in unison to turn those efforts into victories. It is not called a "team game" for nothing.

I can promise you that if you want to stretch out for a higher level of performance, it goes beyond talent and ability. The road to top-notch athletic status is littered with gifted players who came up short of where their abilities indicated they could go. They failed to master the mindset these winning traits can produce to reach super athletic status.

Winning The "Head" Game

Here's a great point that I don't want you to miss: Maybe you will not be good enough to reach the next level as an athlete. However, what you learn as you strive to reach the next level is the kind of mindset needed to excel in other areas of life. The business world is full of former athletes who brought that mindset into their careers. There is no place where sports ends and life outside of sports begins. At the end of one is the beginning of the other.

So many former athletes make great strides in the outside world because they know what it takes to be successful. They have a great work ethic and learn how to put in the effort. Because they have created great performance habits, applying them to the work world is just a natural step.

That brings to mind something quality athletes do that average athletes fail to do. They put in extra time and practice to perfect their skills. This attitude may not have always improved them, but I guarantee it did not make them worse. Your challenge is to wake up every morning hungry to get better. Soon it becomes a habit. It becomes a part of you. It's no longer something you do…it's who you are.

Chapter Eleven

HANGING TOUGH

> Hanging tough is cut from the fabric of persistence and woven with perseverance. There are no areas in athletics immune to this combination...you will go as far as your stay-ability will allow you to go.

BE READY FOR ADVERSITY

Imagine what it would be like if you went through your sports career never encountering any adversity or obstacles. That might sound good, but it is not realistic. The struggles you face in sports make you the athlete you become. If you are not tested or face resistance, how do you grow?

If your basic outlook accepts that unusual negative things are a natural part of sports, this will undoubtedly make you more mentally prepared when adversity does arise. How you view adversity is crucial. Without a certain degree of tolerance and understanding of adverse situations, they can appear to be eternal and never-ending.

Murphy's Law says, *"When something can go wrong, a time will arise when it will."* Too many of us, when the occasion occurs where something adverse happens, create a shock condition leading to extreme mental uneasiness. Consequently, the depth of the feelings experienced when things get out of whack depends on how ready we are to face it on our terms.

Winning The "Head" Game

Plan. Prepare. Practice. That's the route to being ready for things that can get off track. Practice time is the time to prepare for what might go wrong and other unexpected occurrences that might arise during play. Your mind will be much more capable of handling adverse situations when you do everything possible to acquaint yourself with them. Second, mentally, consider adversity a challenge you are always ready to take on.

Adversity can define you depending on how you respond to it. However, it also offers the potential to refine and improve you as you work your way through it—not around it, but through it.

> *"It is easy to conclude that something is over when things look bleak. Yet an essential part of developing a champion's mentality is to hang in there when the going gets tough, and success appears out of sight."*
> Dr. Ken Blanchard

> *"If it is worth doing, it is worth doing wrong."*
> -Tom Peters

> *"You are what you are when the going gets tough."*
> -Yogi Berra

> *"Tough times never last, but tough people do."*
> -Knute Rockne

> *"To never admit making mistakes enhances the chances of making them again."*
> -Adolph Rupp

> *"A loss does not define your team, but what happens next will."*
> -Bill Walton

> *Mistakes are reasons for growth...*
> *not excuses for giving up.*

> **Sometimes, you can get knocked off your feet by something beyond your control. But when you get knocked down, you still have the responsibility to get up. Remember no one is ever a loser by getting knocked down...they only become a loser if they don't get back up-- and do your best to stay up!**

Please don't get discouraged when things have gone about as wrong as they can go. Hang in there--stay the course, and you will emerge a wiser and stronger player on the other side.

A mistake is not a mistake if you learn something from it.

There will always be something from the previous action left within you. Each new beginning carries with it a lesson from things that have happened to you in the past.

"An eraser is not for those who make mistakes... it is for those willing to correct their mistakes."
-Source unknown

Great progress emerges from great challenges.

"Something outside of you can stop you temporarily, only you can do it permanently."
-Frank Beamer

The height of success you attain will be measured by how much adversity you can take before calling it quits.

NO CHALLENGES...NO GLORY

How good are you at hanging in there when the going gets tough and the outcome is unclear? Do the challenges you face draw out the very best within you?

Challenges in any phase of athletics give you glimpses of yourself that you may have never seen. They give you a chance to see what you are made of. They rush to your aid qualities which you may have never known you possess. Challenges allow you to be better than you have been...if you face up to them.

A truism in sports is there is no measure of gain without pain...no, triumphs without trials...no, victories without battles...no peaks without valleys...no glory without challenges. Speaking of valleys, Coach Bobby Bowden reminds us that *"The fertilizer that helps us do our best growing is found in the valley, not on the mountaintop."*

If you have built strong habits of persistence and of mental discipline, you will be aided by these virtues when you face tough challenges. If you have prepared yourself to face challenging situations with courage and conviction, the chances are good that you will enjoy significant rewards. Note that the challenges you face and work to overcome today are developing the courage and strength that makes tomorrow's challenges easier to face.

> *To overcome a difficult challenge doesn't create a "hero," it just brings to the surface the hero that is already present.*
> -Source unknown

> *It is easy to conclude that something is over when things look bleak. Yet an essential part of developing a champion's mentality is to hang in there when the going gets tough and success appears out of sight."*
> -Les Brown

Sonny Smith and Lou Vickery

The Real Test

The test of athletes is the fight they make,
    The grit that they daily show;
The way they stand on their feet and take
    The opponent's toughest blow;
Anyone can do well when there's nothing to fear,
    When nothing, their progress bars;
But it takes real athletes to stand and cheer
    When other athletes are the stars.
The sweet taste of victory comes after all,
    To the athletes who can make
A courageous stand with backs to a wall;
    The ones who can give and take,
And always hold their heads up high –
    Even when bruised and pale;
For this is the athletes who will always try,
    Because they are not afraid to fail.
It is when they decide to make a stand –
    And have courage to remain strong
When victory appears almost at hand,
    That will decide who will win the game.
For the real test of athletes mettle and worth
    Is to fight just one more round.
And ultimately, how they do in the arena,
    Is decided by standing their ground.
    --Adapted from an Unknown Source

Keep going even when quitting would appear the most likely choice.

"You will always perform at a high peak when you discipline yourself to focus on doing your best every time you have an opportunity as if it were going to be the first—and the last time you will ever see it."
-Tony Robbins

Winning The "Head" Game

Too Soon to Quit

Some have told you it can't be done,
Maybe you have thought them right;
But the time will come to move ahead,
Because somehow you think you might.
In the beginning losses may be too many,
Putting to the supreme test your grit;
But a little voice will say: "Stay with it,
Hang in there, it's too soon to quit!"
So, you raised your sights a bit higher,
And charged up with a brand-new will;
You dug your heels in a little deeper,
Because you have big dreams to fulfill.
Then the day arrived to your surprise,
You did what others said couldn't be done;
For you had learned it's too soon to quit,
And with that attitude, by golly you won!   -
Adapted from an unknown author

"The toughest person to beat, is the one who doesn't know the meaning of quit."
-Jim Valvano

"Today's mighty oak is yesterday's little nut who held its ground."
-Josh Billings

G.rit

U.nder

T.ough

S.ledding

A real factor in winning is the ability to hang on where others tend to let go. A more significant factor is your ability to hang on when you want to let go.
-Source unknown

Sonny Smith and Lou Vickery

"The greatness of an individual's strength is the measure of that individual's tendency to surrender."
-General George Patton

> **"When you think you have done all you can and want to give in; Please be reminded that winners don't quit, and quitters don't win."**
> **-Source Unknown**

"Remember the person who gave up? Neither does anyone else."
-Bud Grant

"There is no defeat except within; unless you are defeated there, you'll find a way to win."
-William Danforth

"You have to love the person whose heart is bursting with a passion to overcome."
-Gordie Howe

It takes a lot of heart, nerve and fortitude to hang in there when things go very wrong, and you have very little to cling to, except a little voice telling you to "HOLD ON!"
-Source unknown

> *"Nothing in the world can take the place of persistence. Talent will not; nothing is more common than unsuccessful men with talent. Genius will not: unrewarded genius is almost a proverb. Education will not: the world is full of educated derelicts. Persistence and determination alone are omnipotent."*
> -Calvin Coolidge

Persistence is the ability to keep going when it would be best if you kept going; after you think you have done about all you can do.

> Deep down on the inside, you are not a quitter...you don't give up at the first sign of trouble...you are willing to deny yourself easy exits because you know you have what it takes to hang tough. You know, if you keep working and keep believing, you will emerge stronger and wiser on the other side and know what it is like to be a top athlete.

Keep Yogi Berra's great quote in mind:
"It ain't over until it's over."

A SONNY MOMENT

Anyone who's ever played sports for any length of time knows there is never a time when you "throw in the towel" and start thinking about the next game. Don't give up until the final whistle blows or the match is over. Play every point, play, or down like it matters. You keep fighting—even if losing seems inevitable.

So, never give in, regardless of the score. Keep playing as hard and efficient as you possibly can. When you give up, you regret it afterwards...and if it is a contact sport, you are more accessible to injury. The fewer concessions you make to any opponent, the better you will feel about yourself going forward.

When you "throw in the towel" and begin to go through the motions, you forfeit any chance for victory. I have seen this over the years: a team is more apt to quit when it is the team favored to win and finds itself hopelessly behind on the score. Players become frustrated and upset with what has happened and fail to keep a forward-looking approach that might lead to a big rally and possibly pulling out a win.

    Comebacks happen. Opponents can get complacent with a big lead and start making mistakes. If a team continues to play hard and aggressively, it could be the catalyst that leads to snatching victory from the jaws of defeat. You never know what might happen if you keep scrambling and fighting so long as time remains on the play clock. Superb athletes know all about big comebacks and underdogs defeating heavily favored opponents.

Chapter Twelve

FAIL (LOSE) FORWARD

Admirable as the ideal of winning every time is, no one can win them all. Losing happens…but what counts when a team loses is how team members mentally react to losing.

The price is high because what each player on the team thinks after a loss is often the determining factor in how long it takes to disconnect from the loss and bounce back.

Before a team can learn what consistently winning is all about, it must first learn how to lose. It must learn how to quickly bounce back after a loss—notably one where everyone on the team knew they should have won.

> *"Failure can be defined as a wrong that leaves an impression that turns you in toward yourself. To come up on the short end of the score has no consequences going forward, unless you let it deter you from moving on to the next challenge."*
>
> Dr. Bob Everhart

Winners are not the ones who shy away from losing, nor the ones who never lose, but rather the ones who move forward—who go on in spite of setbacks, learning lessons that minimize the chances of losing…again.

The first thing that should come from losing is the feeling that you don't like it.

UNTANGLE THE TANGLED

Life is full of difficulties, setbacks, and missteps. So is athletics. One of the things that will help you reach championship athlete status is to learn how to sort out the past mysteries of sports. Mentally, you see your difficulties as stepping stones rather than stumbling blocks.

One of the first things you can do to untangle the tangled is to let go of those less-than-successful moments experienced in the past. Champion athletes have learned how to strip away all the accumulative layers of negative things that have happened.

Of course, you still remember those bad events. There's nothing wrong with simply remembering those negatives that were part of your past, but remembering them and dwelling on them are two different things. The key is how to use your "forgettery," we will discuss later, and put those memories in cold storage forever.

Top athletes have discovered the past has passed, so it is no use mulling it over in the mind. Nothing can be done to change what has happened, but there is definitely something that can be captured from it to brighten the future.

How about you? Do you think of the primary and essential premise of the positive benefits and lessons setbacks can almost certainly provide? Within each adverse event is the innate potential of something outstanding. It may be hidden, but it is there. The challenge is to unfold the great treasures of potentiality within the "negatives" you experience.

Once you understand how to benefit from the past, you can move on to the next level in your growth and development. Discard the misstep, setback, or loss. It is a thing of the past. It is time to move on, to stretch out, and to reach a new level of growth.

Okay. How do you untangle the tangled? You must trust your own nature to untangle where you may have been all tangled up thinking of the "negatives" in the past. You need to do two things with the past: learn from it, then run from it.

USE YOUR "FORGETTERY"

Did you and your teammates do everything possible to secure a win, and didn't? What happens now? The suggestion would be to let it hurt for a while--feel the sting, learn the lesson—then move on.

Sometimes, it's the moving on part that is difficult. Earlier, we talked about the use of your *forgettery*. We believe it is a viable trait to possess in athletics. Your *"forgettery"* is one of the greatest weapons to put an error, setback, or loss in the rearview mirror and move on to what's next on the schedule.

The secret of moving on is to let things come and go, using your *"forgettery"* to move on and prepare for your next challenge. This doesn't mean you are suppressing things or being carried away by them, but you are doing your best to learn from the situations and prepare for the next opponent or challenge.

Yet, isn't there a tendency to keep thinking about what should have been done or could have been done to win? Anytime a lousy performance remains front and center in your thoughts, there is a good chance it will affect the subsequent performance…and then the next.

A real outcome of having a good "forgettery" is that it conserves mental energy. Total concentration on what's to come is not easy if the thought process remains on what has happened in the past. This results in mental tiredness, which makes individual team members increasingly more prone to mistakes and failure.

Utilizing your "forgettery" helps to keep things on an even keel, neutralizing the tendency of emotional swings. It leads to a greater balanced approach, where the past is put into the past.

Winning the mental struggle after any loss centers largely around having a good "forgettery." Those with a good "forgettery" enjoy greater success than those who fail to stay focused on the challenge faced in the now moment.

After a loss, the biggest concern is not what happened but what the team members think of it. A team's weak moments are only as strong as memories of them.

RECOVERY CAPACITY

Hopefully, we have distinguished that failure to do something that should or could have been done is a great learning force. That depends on whether you are up to the task of learning from it and applying what you have learned to produce better future results.

Winning develops in an environment where a team maximizes its use of its *forgettery* and then utilizes the power of its recovery capacity. Recovery capacity centers on a team's ability to bounce back by focusing on the "teachable moment" losing creates.

A unified recovery capacity results in more productive efficiency for individual players and the team. The sustainability of the recovery depends in great part on the team's resiliency.

The critical element of a team's recovery capacity is the focus is not on what has happened but on what can happen. Lessons to be learned occur quickly and more readily when a team's recovery capacity is open to constructive instruction. Through this openness, a team can understand what it takes to win and move on to the next game with increased vigor and mental acumen.

Fail Forward Lessons

- When you lose, don't lose the lesson.
- A star shines the brightest in the dark.

It doesn't take any talent to be a quitter.

- Mistakes are lessons…. not failure.
- If you don' think about quitting – you won't.

You can never be a winner acting like a loser.

- New beginnings can only come from old endings.
- When things go wrong, don't go wrong with things.
- How we exit will be remembered longer than how we entered.
- Weak moments are only as strong as memories of them.

- *Forgettery* is just as important to success as is memory.

Don't act like you are defeated, defeat is certain then.

- It takes power to endure the effects of failure… and guts to make the effort to overcome it.
- Don't ever talk like a failure—failure is certain then.
- Defeat is bitter only if we swallow it.
- Every great improvement we make in life comes after we have failed.
- Always "fail forward." Never look at a failure or loss in any other way than as a fulcrum for learning—that will facilitate coming out on the other side smarter.

> **All human beings fail on occasion. And since you are a human being you are going to fail, which means you are only human. Right?**

OTHER THOUGHTS

To be successful, every team participant and coach must make losing a breeding ground where everyone learns what it takes to be more successful. Since losing in the pursuit of winning is a given, you and your teammates must strive to loss forward.

Here are other "loss forward" thoughts:

- Failure is simply a mental process…a state of mind.
- Think: *"When a team fails, it doesn't make it a failure. It is just a learning experience…and nothing more."*
- A team will best be remembered by the times it succeeds--not by the times it fails.
- When a team comes up short, it is important that players not personalize it and put themselves down. A team wins

together. A team loses together. The best policy is always to try to *"separate you from what you do."*

- Let the past -- pass. A loss only affects the next opportunity when the team holds on to the last poor one.

"Moving beyond a loss begins with controlling the one aspect of losing that is in each participant's hand... controlling their own thoughts about the loss."
-Dean Smith

"You will never be a winner acting like a loser...
and the more comfortable you become
with losing, the easier losing is."
-Nick Saban

*"Things work out for the best when you
make the best of the way things work out."*
-Pat Head Summit

> **Your ability to win is only as great as your capacity to handle losing. Even the best lose... but what makes them different is what happens after a loss. Winners are not the ones who shy away from losing or who never lose, but rather the ones who move forward—who go on in spite of setbacks, learning lessons that minimize the chances of losing again.**

"The road to success always has detour signs along the traveling route. It's a long try-way, not an easy road way."
-Zig Ziglar

*To admit that you were less than your best is
a sign of strength–not a confession of weakness.*

LOSER'S LIMP

Anyone who has competed in sports for any length of time knows what a "loser's limp" looks like. For those who may not have heard the term "loser's limp," it is where a player acts out an injury after blowing a big play or failing miserably against a lesser opponent.

We would like to have a dollar for every time we saw this through the years; a player has a chance to score a big goal, and misses. He then begins to limp in "pain," looking for the crowd to say, *"Gracious, he would have surely scored but for that injury."*

Maybe the fans genuinely believed he had an injury, but what about the player himself? How about his teammates? The player knows by feigning an injury, he may manage to save face in front of the fans. They possibly believe his inability to perform at a peak level was because of the injury, but deep down the player himself knows better--he knows he blew it.

A player who employs a *"loser's limp,"* loses the respect of his coaches and teammates, notably when it becomes a fairly consistent occurrence. However, the fact remains that the player didn't execute when the chips were down.

We would venture that it is human to want to provide the rationale for poor performance by placing the blame on something or someone else. It happens to coaches as well as individual players. How many referees or umpires have been blamed for a loss? That is always a convenient excuse. It is still a "loser's limp" in our book.

To use the ready-made excuse of a "loser's limp," never changes the outcome. It never makes anything better, either. Our experience has been that the further up the success ladder a team or an athlete climbs, the less they use a "loser's limp" as an excuse for poor results.

Everyone fails to execute on occasion. Yet, if something on the outside is always responsible when things get off track, there is little desire and ambition to truly address the internal challenges.

Everyone associated with a team needs to forego relying on a crutch in tough situations.

A couple of questions: If a team and its players are never held accountable for their shortcomings, how can they improve? What is there to improve on if a team is not willing to forego excuses for poor results and undertake a process of making workable adjustments?

The rule is simple: *"If you mess up, fess up."* You can never find a solid step on the winners' ladder if you spend time searching for excuses. To move on beyond a "loser's limp," ask yourself this question: *"What am I doing about the one thing I can improve? What am I doing about me?"*

> **Nothing inhibits progress more than making excuses and passing the blame. The moment a team searches for an excuse--any excuse--is when the team limits its possibilities for future success. Relying on excuses for shortcomings does nothing to change those faults. Please understand that the further up the success ladder a team hopes to climb, the less it will search for—and make-- excuses for poor performance.**

"You can think about ways to win or keep from losing. While the former does not always guarantee winning, the latter pretty much guarantees losing."
-Bum Phillips

Think: "When I fail, it is not failure. It is just a learning experience... and nothing more."

"You will rarely find a place on the leaderboard if you always search for excuses for poor performance or mistakes. A loser's limb is the forerunner to losing."
-Arnold Palmer

PROCESS OF LOSING FORWARD

The one thing that sets champions apart is their ability to use setbacks to grow from them. They maintain this supportive feeling even if they give their best effort and come up short. It gives them more determination to right the ship and seek the next challenge. The lessons taught by those occasions when they have a lack of success are the driving force helping champions refine and strengthen efforts as they advance.

The "Loss forward" process involves three stages:

1. AWARENESS STAGE. *"I should not be doing... (whatever needs to be done differently)."*

2. ACCEPTANCE STAGE. *"I should be doing... (options of what you should be doing)."*

3. ACTION STAGE. *"I will... (specify what you will do to bring improvement to your performance)."*

> **What counts when a team loses is how team members react to losing. The price is high because it is not the regrettable loss that carries the highest value but the thought process you and your teammates have about it. The key factor is how long it takes for the team to mentally recover and get back on the road toward preparing for the next opponent.**

A real understanding of what happened after it happened, provides a path to learn those things that enable you to make something more promising happen.

The (team) cannot go back again to the place where it started and make a brand-new beginning ... but the (team) can start where it is now and make a brand-new ending."
　　　　　　　　　　-Stephen Covey

HEADS...UP

So, you lost. Got the stuffing knocked out of you, did you? What is your normal posture after you experience defeat? Head down with shoulders slumped, right? The head position is body language personified. A great reminder: *"Let me see your eyes."*

Do you realize it's mentally impossible to walk around thinking negatively with your head up and eyes open? To think negatively, you have to drop your head, or even close your eyes. Head down is the position where you begin to think about all the "bad things" that have happened or you envision will happen.

Every emotion has its corresponding physical counterpart. Something great happens when you lift your head, square your shoulders, and erect your body. These physical acts trigger biological processes that alter the mind's perception of what it is *"supposed to feel."* Your thoughts focus on positivity.

Keep your head up and your eyes level when things are not going your way. This simple act will help you focus on what lies ahead and keep you positively focused on doing your best right where you are.

"During any competitive event, a team should always perform so that if it fails to come out on top, every team member should walk away feeling like the competitors succeeded more than they failed."
-Dr. Marv Levy

WINNING GIVES CLUES

This chapter has distinguished the importance of learning the lessons arising from defeat. We will close this chapter by discussing winning and the clues it provides for improving future performance and results.

What do you and your teammates need to do to continue climbing the success ladder in the fashion you have demonstrated? Winning consistently has built-in clues as to what must be done to continue along that path. There are lessons in winning, just like there

Winning The "Head" Game

are in losing. The key is to look at winning as a building block. There are always signs in winning that point out ways to improve.

Regardless of how high you and your teammates are on the success ladder, there are always things to learn to help you improve. You must constantly evolve and improve your body of work. It should be ingrained in your daily habits.

KEEP EVOLVING

Winning ways can easily be reversed unless a team constantly aims higher, breaks through new barriers, uses more productive ways to perform, and strives for winning results every time it enters a competitive event or takes on a new challenge. The record book is full of teams that let their press clippings get in the way of consistently producing quality results.

A given in sports is that those with more drive and ambition will knock a team off its pedestal if they are not working hard to improve. So, regardless of where a team is on the success ladder, no one--coaches or players alike--can ever afford to feel like they can show up and win. A realism of competition is that a team with more desire and purpose will knock the cockiness right out of a team full of themselves, dropping them right down on their knees.

Just for the record, please understand that winning is never final, and losing is never fatal. Keep on striving to be on the winning side of the scorecard.

"The most important thing that comes from winning are not things."
-Lavell Edwards

RESULTS-ORIENTED

A results-oriented attitude is vital to winning the "head game," notably after a defeat. It is crucial to the level of your play that you have a healthy, ongoing attitude toward obtaining the results that help put you and your team on the winning side. Here's our take on results: *"Results IS your greatest asset."*

When you focus energy on the results you want and expect, the brain is treated with an injection of *dopamine*. This is the chemical that makes us look forward to repeating winning experiences. Think about that: A healthy attitude toward results influences the actions that lead to obtaining those results. Each time you anticipate you can obtain quality results, you are more apt to be endowed with the resources to achieve a positive outcome.

No doubt, a results-oriented attitude will lead you in a winning direction. You will tend to see opportunities where other players fail to see them. It will be a guiding light in helping you to develop the fortitude to move through and over obstacles that possibly would stop less results-oriented players.

Never underestimate your personal attitude's role in the results the team obtains. Winning is the accumulation of a team's collective thoughts, attitude, and efforts. Winning results is the ultimate barometer of all things in athletics.

Two Winning Ends

You have two winning ends,
They have a common link...
With the bottom end you move...
With the top end you think.
And winning truly depends on
How you maximize their use;
For common sense dictates–
With both, you win--one, you lose.
-Adapted from an unknown author

A SONNY MOMENT

You probably have not considered this, but there are learning opportunities when you win or lose. Here's my rule: When you lose, learn from it. When you win, learn from it. Show up every day ready to improve.

Winning The "Head" Game

Athletic success is about making progress from game to game. As we know, a team is not always successful, but with the right mindset, it can always make the best of any defeat.

When a team is prospering and everything is going the right way, a coach may have to take the necessary steps to avoid an air of arrogance and haughtiness that can creep into a locker room. If you are not careful, a team can be too cocky and over-confident by good fortune, just as much so as by being less excited and lacking in self-confidence by the bad. Keeping a team on an even keel is constant, notably when the team is learning how to win.

I probably practiced my teams a tad harder when we were on a winning streak than when we were not enjoying higher success. I often thought that losing was more apt to occur after a big win, so I preached we should take the path as coaches to focus on practicing harder than expected.

Think through what I am going to say now. Winning is important, but losing may be more critical. Think about that for a minute. You see, losing engenders negative feelings and consequences, and given enough time and pressure, it leads to a general downward spiral for a team. In some situations, it often leads to the same within a community. For better or worse, sports have become essential in communities nationwide.

My feeling is that the priority is to find ways to avoid losing. Elsewhere in the book, you will find this quote: *"The best thing that should come from losing is the feeling you don't like it."* When that kind of attitude permeates a team, it has taken a step toward finding ways to avoid losing.

Developing a winning culture is no easy task. Winning is by design, not by accident. The road to winning (and losing for that matter) is always under construction.

Recognizing that the architect of a winning culture will produce a very different path. That path begins with concentrating on a positive environment of words and actions.

This book has focused on that. The insight in these pages sustains and further reflects upon the continuous flow of positive-building activity, which portrays winning as a destination and a journey. In that regard, every moment, every minute, every hour, every day a coach or player is involved in an athletic endeavor, the focus is on developing a winning culture.

Pay attention to everything that is happening now with consciously heightened awareness. A winning culture may not come immediately. It may only look like a good idea. But if you focus on the present, there is an opportunity—there is a possibility.

That's right. The critical factor is to realize that winning is encoded in the here and now. It is always now that you should be thinking about doing what it takes to be a winner—not earlier, not later, yesterday, or tomorrow, but right now. Center your attention on fully and completely investing in this moment, focusing on winning thoughts as if it were your only moment. Winning is a consequence of something in the present. You build a more favorable foundation for the future.

While now is the result of all your yesterdays and the basis of all your tomorrows, the wise decision is to put the past behind you. Appreciate that you are the result of your past. But your present actions and words have implications for the future. Your ability to move on depends on keeping the present front and center.

A brighter future is on the horizon. It has not arrived yet, but it is on its way. The only ground you can stand on is the present. Even contemplating the future or the past is a function of present awareness. Lean heavily on that part of you, ready to visualize—creatively and expansively—the possible instead of the impossible. An essential step in this process is to expand your awareness. Awareness will allow you to come alive to the greatness you have within.

Chapter Thirteen

EMOTIONAL CONTROL

Others cannot make you lose emotional control, only you can do that to yourself.

Do you tend to lose your temper when things don't go your way? Do you fly off the handle when someone does something or says something you don't like? Do you quickly become angry with yourself when you are not performing as well as you know that you can? Unless you maintain a firm grip on these emotions, they can carry you further and further away from the mainstream of an enjoyable and successful athletic career.

As you probe your experiences, what can you say about the role emotions play in your sports experience and life? How are you doing in the area of emotional control and stability? Are your emotions working for or against you? Are your emotions your best servant or your worst enemy?

Experiencing the breadth and depth of emotions comes with the territory in sports. Almost everything that happens before, during, and after a game is interpreted at the emotional level.

The word "emotion" comes from the Latin word "exmovere," meaning *"to excite, stir up or to move."* Emotions are a basic and essential part of being human. There is little question that emotional control is a vital priority for playing sports and maximizing your budding career as a player.

We are convinced that a high *emotional quotient* (EQ) in athletics will advance an athlete up the success ladder almost as surely as a high IQ. Both are needed; because, the nature of sports calls for emotional control and stability both on and off the field.

EVEN KEEL

It takes a concise mental effort to develop an earnest and steadfast outlook that allows you to remain undisturbed in times of emotional stress. By not caving into highly emotional situations, you enjoy a better presence of mind and clarity of judgment as you tackle your responsibilities. It is in this frame of mind that you perform your best.

Do you need help attaining an efficient state of emotional control? If so, the first and most crucial step in this fact-gathering process is understanding situations that create emotional extremes.

Armed with this awareness, you can consciously work to balance these expanded emotional boundaries. You can focus fully on tackling those emotional situations where you tend to lose control. Awareness is the beginning. Following that up with action, or possibly inaction, is the next step, whichever is the case.

Participating and performing with poise regularly is possible where your emotions work for you, not against you. Make more productive emotions a part of your in-game activity going forward. Your need for conscious awareness lessens as you become more habitual in your effort to abate extreme emotional reactions. Eventually, it becomes second nature. But there is no shortcut. You must be vigilant at all times to keep emotions in line.

We hope you hear us saying that top performers do not get too overcharged. They have a calmness and ease about themselves that helps them maintain emotional equilibrium in pressure cooker-type situations that are a significant part of any sport. They exercise composure in situations where constraint is vital to achievement.

It is possible to participate and perform at a high level with emotions working for you and not against you. Once you have become fully and consciously aware of how you respond when you have experienced a tendency to lose control, you can work toward more productive emotions being a part of your activity as you advance. The need for conscious awareness lessens as you become habitual in your effort to curtail emotional reactions.

EMOTIONAL INHIBITORS

Speaking of negative emotions, over six hundred words found in the dictionary express negative feelings. Consequently, negative emotions are part of sports. For some, they tend to dominate thought patterns. We hope that's not you. The depth of the reaction you internalize about negative situations could lead to unhealthy choices and consequences.

Unpleasant feelings are just as crucial as enjoyable ones in helping a player get a handle on the ups and downs of sports. If it weren't for a few negative emotions now and then, you wouldn't enjoy the good ones as much, would you?

A word of caution: Attempting to suppress negative emotions can backfire and even diminish a sense of well-being. Instead of backing away from negative emotions, you must accept and manage them. How you deal with emotions, especially negative ones, has significant consequences. Emotions come. Emotions go. The key is the aftermath. Some negative emotions can take you to depths that create negative issues.

Generally, it is essential to avoid emotional extremes, notably during game action. Highly emotional actions, when carried to extremes, can become a source of harm for a team. How often have you seen a player celebrate after executing a great play, only to lose focus and get burned on the next play?

This may make us look like we are too "old school" to appreciate the emotional excitement that players today exhibit after making a great play. Celebration is okay as long as you don't lose sight of the fact it was just one play. It is our experience the best athletes expect to make great plays, so rarely do they undergo excessive celebratory reactions when they do. They turn their attention to the forthcoming action. The best athletes seldom exhibit emotional reactions which end up hurting their team. They are vigilant at all times to keep negative emotions in line.

Positive emotions are healthy for attaining and maintaining mental stability. Conversely, research shows that effectively handling negative emotions plays a vital role in your and the team's well-being.

If your inability to handle "negatives" concerns you, set a goal of working harder to gain a more outstanding grip on handling harmful emotions. In those situations where you have experienced difficulty in maintaining effective emotional control, be solution-minded. What follows are tactics and techniques to assist you in creating more emotional balance.

*The more you manage yourself from within,
the less you need to be managed from without.*

RELAXATION

The ability to relax is a key factor in handling those "emotional-type situations." Relaxation is a process that decreases the effects of emotional stress and anxiety on your mind and body. Many outstanding athletes have cut their careers short because they cannot handle elevated emotional conditions. Over time, the tension generated by stress hurts their bodies, leading to injury and various health issues.

We firmly believe that adequately employing relaxation techniques can help you cope with pre-game and stress-related game situations. Relaxation may be as crucial to improving athletic performance as any undertaking. You can benefit from learning relaxation techniques if you tend to get uptight and experience severe "butterflies" before a game.

Relaxation is a skill. You can train your mind and body to do it. Learning basic relaxation techniques is simple and easy. As with any form of skill development, relaxation techniques improve with practice. You can find them all over the internet.

Two thoughts before moving on to the techniques: First, be patient with yourself. Don't let your effort to practice relaxation techniques become another stress source. Second, try another method if one relaxation technique doesn't work for you. We discuss three here:

Winning The "Head" Game

Visualization: In this relaxation technique, you visualize taking A trip where your focus is on your role and the activity you will be engaged in, not on the results of that activity. The results you want will be there when you clear your mind of excess tension, relax, and visualize successfully performing your role and making all the right moves.

This is an excellent technique to use pre-game. You may want to close your eyes, sit in a quiet spot, loosen any tight clothing, and listen to soothing music. The aim is to focus on the present and visualize positive actions.

Muscle Relaxation: In this relaxation technique, you focus on slowly tensing and then relaxing each muscle group. This can help you understand the difference between muscle tension and normal relaxation.

Muscle relaxation starts by tensing and relaxing the muscles in groups from your toes to your head. You can also start with your head and neck and work down to your toes. Focus on tensing your muscles for about five seconds, then relax for 30 seconds, and repeat.

Deep Breathing: When you feel a "rush" racing through your body, there is an ageless but simple breathing exercise that can dissipate mental and physical stress. While deep breathing is typically incredibly beneficial for the body, many see it as a great way to relax the mind, even more so than the body.

You can use three dimensions to improve your relaxation ability through proper deep breathing. The first lesson is to shut your mouth. Secondly, slowly draw in a good deep breath through your nose. Then, thirdly, exhale slowly through your mouth. The pace at which you breathe and how you breathe will enhance your ability to relax in tense situations.

Relax and remember this too shall pass...
Peace of mind holds you in good stead all the time.

> **Balance reason with emotion. Balance your reactions to the things happening around you and within you—whether good or bad.**

Learn to check tendencies toward becoming overly emotional in those situations where strong emotional reactions are prevalent.

"IT'S OKAY" ATTITUDE

The first law in tackling any challenge is to view it as being okay.

One of the best ways to maximize emotional control is to key in on an "It's okay" attitude. This attitude is built on the premise that if you can do nothing about a situation, why should you get emotionally involved?

Few of us are immune to the little things that can get under our skin and endanger our emotional well-being. How do you react when a teammate doesn't do what they said they were going to do…you are late for practice, and the driver in front of you is going ten miles below the speed limit…that misassignment the coach got in your face about? Did you get internally upset and react emotionally? Does blowing your stack change any of these conditions? We doubt it.

Isn't it really okay for the world to move at its own pace? If you get upset, what have you achieved? What have you truly accomplished with this kind of action? The only thing you accomplish is letting someone or something consciously or unconsciously knock you right out of an "It's okay" state of mind.

You can get upset, angry, and miserable, but guess what? It doesn't change the reality of the situation. The same holds true for worry. When you worry, you visualize the problem, not the solution. By picturing an issue continuously in the mind, you get more worry. Worry gives you something to do, but it won't get you anywhere. The truth is that worry is just a big bluff.

When we allow our problems to be okay, we have positioned ourselves to move beyond the problem and begin seeking an answer or solution. The goal is simple: adjust to the realities of life, regardless of how unfair these realities appear to be. An "It's okay" attitude helps us realize that if there is nothing we can do about circumstances, we will not let it concern us.

A roommate of mine (Lou) in pro baseball often used the term, *"You gotta cooperate with the inevitable."* Learn to go with the flow. Let things be. *"Cooperate with the inevitable."* Establish an "It's okay" attitude. If you do, you will last longer and go further.

KEEP YOUR COOL

We are not making light of *"keeping your cool,"* but here are some humorous ideas from various unknown sources that can help:

- The more you grow up, the less you will blow up.
- Flying into a rage always results in unsafe landings.
- Those who are always exploding rarely end up being big shots.
- It's more tasteful to swallow angry words before we say them…than to eat them afterward.
- Those who lose their heads are the last to realize it.
- We are more apt to remain calm and collected when we restrain from shooting from the lip.
- We contribute to the world's pollution problem when we blow our stacks.
- The trouble with letting off steam is that it only gets us into more hot water.
- Others find out what kind of minds we have when we give them a piece of it.
- Before giving someone a piece of your mind, ensure you can get by with what's left.

"BUTTERFLIES"

The emotional experience that really stands out is the pre-game "butterflies" which buzz around in your stomach prior to a game. The "butterflies" arise from the feeling you are excited and ready to get the game started.

Whatever you do, refrain from thinking of those flutters in your stomach as a fundamental and functional negative factor. There's a tendency to misinterpret this case of "nerves" pessimistically. You might begin to question whether you are capable of matching up with your opponent, or if you are adequately prepared to compete.

Think of the "butterflies" you experience as a plus. They are great servants. They work on your behalf. They are a positive sign that you are mentally and physically ready to perform. So, don't fight the "butterflies." Let them work for you... not against you.

TAKING THINGS IN STRIDE

As we close this chapter, it is worth to look at some things that will help to fight emotional disparities:

- Manage time wisely. Control your time rather than your time controlling you, aids greatly in balancing emotions.
- Focus on solutions. When you look beyond your problems, you see a world of opportunity.
- Prepare for key events. Preparing mentally, emotionally, and physically for important events helps you to stay calm in those situations where tension tends to ride high.
- Laughter is therapeutic. Use humor to your advantage. Laughter relieves tension and overwhelming feelings.
- Don't try to be a perfectionist. Strive for excellence. Being excellent will significantly reduce your emotions.
- Keep an eye on your emotions when you are in motion.
- Remind yourself that a "It's okay" attitude is essential.

Chapter Fourteen

A HEALTHIER YOU

Those who are good are often separated from those who are great by their readiness to perform.

A guarantee in any competitive venue like sports is there comes a time when being mentally and physically ready to perform comes into question. If the laws of strenuous workouts, good diet, and proper rest have been taken lightly, the body will be bankrupt of strength when strength is most needed. When the body gives out, it takes one's positive attitude and desires to perform well with it.

> *"Attitude plays a crucial role in overall health. It is the rule, not the exception in physical care. It is not a choice but a necessity to expand the practice of maintaining quality physical conditioning year-round. A positive, optimistic attitude about your body makes it a healthy reality. Nothing will mean more to your success than being physically, mentally, and emotionally ready to perform to the best of your abilities–every time that you are in a competitive athletic situation."*
> -Dr. Bob Weil

"Take care of your body,
you only get one."
-Yogi Berra

"WHAT YOU EAT--YOU ARE"

In the age of fast food, it is often difficult to eat the right food and in the right amount. When you are hungry, willpower takes a back seat, and a fast-food restaurant is nearby. There is often a struggle between your will and temptation. When temptation takes over, we eat more of the wrong kinds of food. Do all you can to let your *will* lead the way.

Eating right is essential to long-term effectiveness as an athlete. It is crucial to be actively conscious of your food and how you eat it. Changing eating habits is no simple task, but it is of genuine importance for any athlete striving to perform at the highest level possible.

It takes mental toughness to change long-time eating patterns. A smart move is to establish a strategy for eliminating bad eating habits. Give these a good trial run:

- STOP TO EAT. When it is time to eat, eat. Drop what you are doing and focus on eating. You will enjoy it more and find that you won't need to eat as much food.

- SIT TO EAT. Eating on the run causes us to grab a snack later on. On the go, we are less aware of how much food we consume. Sit at a table to eat, even if your food arrives in a bag.

- DON'T SHOVEL. Slow down and enjoy your food. You will also experience less bloating. Swallowing air leads to bloating and can create gas. The same occurs when you talk with your mouth full. Take smaller bites, eat slowly, and chew food with closed mouth.

- STOP EATING BEFORE YOU ARE FULL. Put your fork down at the first tinge of fullness. This allows your brain to catch up with the realization you are full before you overeat.

- REDUCE YOUR SNACKS. Do you tend to over-indulge in calorie-laced products between meals? The best rule is to cut back on snacking. It keeps the stomach "turned on," leading to the habit of overeating.

- WATCH WHAT YOU SNACK ON. Okay. If you are a "snacker," let your choice of a snack fall within the 10/5/20 rule. This rule establishes snacks should have no more than 10% fat, 5% carbohydrates, and 20% sugar of daily requirements. Even then, eating snacks always evolves around moderation. Makes sense, doesn't it?

- EAT WITH OTHERS. Research shows eating with others tends to slow down your eating behavior. You also take more time to talk and share. As a result, you eat more slowly, which registers more quickly in the brain that you are full.

"A great way not to overeat is to focus on 'crunch time'. That is the sound we hear as we chew food. It has a ring of 'crunch'. The expert opinion is to 'chew like a cow', which is slow and methodical. The "crunch" sound is a cue--if we listen to it--that tends to make us more aware of regulating how much food we intake."

-Dr. Ted Broer

"More and more research points to the lack of proper nutrition as the cause of many of our health issues. The food you eat and the way you eat will make a significant difference in your energy level and the quality of your performance. It is crucial to your overall health that you be tough with yourself at the food line. Listen to your body. It tells the whole story."

D. P. Vickery

HYDRATION

Drink plenty of liquids—even more if you want to remain hydrated during physical activity. In fact, hydration is essential to peak performance and health safety. When you do not consume enough water or replace enough electrolytes to stay properly hydrated, you can create all kinds of health concerns that can lead to devastating conditions.

Drinking enough water each day has these health reasons:

- regulates body temperature
- helps the heart more easily pump blood
- keeps other organs functioning properly
- maintains body muscle tone
- assists the brain to work efficiently
- aids in digestion
- keeps joints lubricated
- prevents infections
- helps the heart more easily pump blood
- keeps organs functioning properly
- delivers nutrients to cells
- fights fatigue/prolongs endurance
- improves sleep quality

Many of you consume sweetened beverages, which are not the answer to staying hydrated. According to the experts, energy drinks, sodas, vitamin waters, and even too much fruit juice do more harm than good regarding hydration. We probably stepped on a few toes with that bit of information.

Another word of caution: while it is not common, it is possible to drink too much water. When a large amount of water is consumed quickly, it can dilute the sodium levels. Feelings of light-headedness and dizziness are symptoms of too much water too fast. This can also strain the kidneys as they attempt to rid the body of the liquid. **Athletes should drink about a gallon of water per day.**

Winning The "Head" Game

SLEEP

Sleep is vital to your overall health and ability to perform effectively in an athletic environment. During sleep, your body works to support healthy brain function and advance the growth and development of your physical health.

Adequate sleep affects how well you think, react, work, learn, and get along with others. Inadequate rest plays a large role in raising the risk of long-term health problems. Lack of adequate sleep is a big detriment to quality performance. It can also affect the heart, circulatory, respiratory, and immune systems.

How much sleep is enough? Research demonstrates that young athletes need 8 to 10 of sleep to maintain a healthy body. If you are deviating from this requirement, seek advice to help change your sleep pattern.

Here are five steps to more incredible sleep habits that the Mayo Clinic recommends:

Stick to a sleep schedule:

Set aside at least eight hours for sleep. Go to bed and get up simultaneously every day, including on weekends. Being consistent is important in reinforcing your body's sleep-wake cycle. The absence of regular sleep leads to mental lapses throughout the day.

When you have trouble going to sleep:

If you fail to fall asleep within about 20 minutes of going to bed, leave your bedroom and do something relaxing. Read or listen to soothing music. Then go back to bed when you're tired. Repeat as needed but continue as best you can to maintain your regular length of sleep schedule.

Be careful what you eat and drink late:

Don't go to bed hungry or stuffed. In particular, avoid heavy or large meals within a couple of hours of bedtime. Discomfort might keep you awake. The stimulating effects of nicotine and caffeine take hours to wear off and can interfere with sleep. Heavy sweets can affect sleep, as well.

Create a restful and peaceful environment:

Keep your room cool, dark, and quiet. Exposure to light in the evenings might make it more challenging to fall asleep. Avoid prolonged use of light-emitting screens just before bedtime. Consider using room-darkening shades, earplugs, a fan or other devices to create an environment that suits your needs to grab a good night of sleep.

Manage your thoughts:

Try to resolve your worries or concerns before bedtime. Jot down what's on your mind and then set it aside for tomorrow. It will give you something to look forward to.

EXERCISE REGULARLY...FOREVER

Your participation in an exercise program is essential. We play tennis regularly, which gives us the chance to exercise. Walking in between tennis playing is part of our routine. Walking 30 minutes daily is a beneficial form of exercise. Your doctor can help you decide what's best for you. Just add an exercise program to your daily routine. It will help you last longer and go further daily.

What is worth noting is what happens after you begin a regular exercise program...you get into the habit of moving and grooving. The carryover value of the lessons you learn will serve you well in the future.

One of the best benefits of a regular exercise program is its positive effect on maintaining a healthy body. Research shows that exercise can produce a more beneficial cardiovascular system, leading to better blood circulation to the body—even to our brains, improving memory and mental faculties. Exercise also reduces the risk of cancer, high blood pressure, diabetes, and delays aging.

Exercise can also improve appearance. It can keep us looking and feeling younger throughout our entire lives. Posture is notably improved, making muscles firmer and more toned. The simple fact is that you feel better.

"PAUSE FOR THE CAUSE"

Learn to unwind so you will have something in the tank when it is time to wind back up again.

Our goal here has been to raise awareness of athletes' health challenges today. We are not qualified to offer professional, in-depth assistance, but we would like to offer a couple of suggestions.

First, learn the art of doing nothing. That's right, a wise move is to establish a goal-free zone where nothing has been scheduled, where there are no deadlines, responsibilities, or places to be. Such a zone allows you to unwind, regroup, and just be yourself. This is a great tool to get a new perspective on you…and a clearer picture of "What next?" in your life.

A second thing to consider is one of the more difficult things for active people to do: take a *"pause for the cause."* Sometimes you need to slow down and back off, taking some time away from the athletic environment.

Taking a self-restoring timeout is as much about mental gain as it is about physical gain. This "timeout" gives the creative juices a chance to flourish. It allows you to think through ideas and solutions buried under the hustle and bustle of daily activities. One of the most important things you can learn is how to do nothing and when you should do it.

ENERGY

The good old dictionary defines energy: *"The strength and vitality required for sustained physical or mental activity."* One of the first rules of sustained performance is the availability of energized power. Your energy level speaks volumes about you before you ever speak. Energized people stand out from the crowd. Is that you?

Energy is one of those things that you either have or don't have. Your capacity for vigorous activity largely depends on developing your energy level. Energy is a derivative of diet, rest, and workout routines. Without great energy, the extent of your viability to perform with vigor and power from start to finish will be diminished. Don't overlook the importance of energy to getting things done.

What can you do when you feel less energetic to develop more energy? Here are some suggestions:

- THINK ENERGY. The first lesson in releasing energy is to think ENERGY. Within is enough energy to do what you need and what you want to do. All you have to do is to access it. That begins with thinking energy in your less-than-energetic moments, and the first thing you know energy will reappear and rejuvenate you..

- HAVE A SENSE OF PURPOSE. The more you are aligned with your purpose of playing your very best in every game, you will experience an output of greater energy. Being specific about where you are headed and what you want to accomplish will also create the availability of more energy to get it done.

- STAY ACTIVE. Energetic players don't waste their time on unproductive thoughts and activities. They don't sit around using up energy worrying about a coming event. They stay focused on positive outcomes. Their theme is the "more I do, the more I have to do with."

- STIMULATE ENERGY. You can stimulate energy through your body movements and posture. Run places even if you can walk. When you walk, do it at a brisk, purposeful pace. Look alive and alert. Appear dynamic in all of your activities. The key is to remind yourself that you are a bundle of energy.

ENDURANCE

Endurance is one of the main ingredients in sustainable athletic performance. It encompasses two major activity functions: mental endurance and physical endurance. These two forms of endurance create a foundation for sustained activity during high-intensity participation.

Mental endurance describes your brain's ability to continuously engage efficiently and effectively in extremely competitive sports action for as long as needed. Physical endurance is a combination of strength and stamina. It describes how long you can maintain a high level of performance without becoming fatigued and worn out.

The technique and method used in developing mental endurance has one crucial component: focus. No matter how much drive and force you apply during sports activities, endurance is useless if wasted on unproductive activity. Focus on what can make a difference in your regular playing efforts.

Physical endurance is like cardiovascular endurance, but there are differences. Cardiovascular endurance, also known as "cardio development," deals with your heart's and lungs' ability to deliver oxygen to your muscle tissue. The abundance of workout activity adds to "cardio development."

Physical development leads to greater endurance when your heart is strong and actively pumping blood, which results in more energy and less fatigue. Physical endurance addresses an increase in blood flow that enhances the ability to keep on going, augmenting your overall physical well-being.

Chapter Fifteen

PREVENTING SPORTS INJURIES

In this chapter, we will turn the discussion's major thrust over to our friend, Dr. Bob Weil, who hosts the internationally acclaimed radio show THE SPORTS DOCTOR. Dr. Bob is a trained sports podiatrist who has hosted his show for over forty years. Dr. Bob is a 2019 inductee in the prestigious National Fitness HOF and co-author of the best-selling book HEY SPORTS PARENTS.

Youth sports have always been famous for many reasons, and today is no different. Unfortunately, along with all the positive aspects of youth sports, there is an alarming increase in injuries, both physical and mental—especially overuse and repetitive motion injuries. The pandemic multiplied ALL OF IT!

PREVENTION IS KEY!

Sports injuries happen at all ages in sports, including sprains, strains, broken bones, torn tendons, ligaments, and concussions. Many of these are acute injuries that occur suddenly during any sporting activity. However, the pressure to win, overzealous parents, coaches and schedules, year-round participation, and specialization are all reasons for the increased incidence of sports injuries.

Many injuries are attributed to overuse. Some classic examples are young baseball pitchers, swimmers, or tennis players with elbow and shoulder problems. Track and field injuries from running and jumping increase foot, ankle, knee, and back injuries.

These types of injuries are not acute ones that occur suddenly but tend to be chronic and persistent without any specific incident. They are more gradual, insidious, and often more difficult to identify, along with many treatment challenges.

Winning The "Head" Game

Doing too much, too often, too soon, and too aggressively is at the core of youth sports today. Specialization in one sport is a mass concern because it creates repetitive motion injuries at young ages. Using the same muscles the same way for a particular sport contributes to overuse and susceptibility to injury... and often, it leads to burnout.

Parents and coaches need to be keenly aware of these challenges and problems. They must listen and pay close attention to complaints from their young athletes. As I stressed in a previous article on "Youth Sports & Drugs," relying on OTC pain and anti-inflammatory drugs to continue participation is never wise!

Ensuring that persistent soreness or pain complaints are given proper attention is smart! Parents need to ensure their young athletes back off and pay attention to rest, recovery, and adequate evaluation of any injury by medical & physical therapy professionals.

Often, persistent and recurrent overuse problems and injuries such as plantar fasciitis, growth center abuses, shin splints, or knee problems are related to body and foot mechanics. These can be associated with leg length differences, flat feet, high arches, bowed lower legs, and knock knees, so having an evaluation by members of the podiatry, chiropractic, and sports therapy fields is essential, especially if problems recur or persist.

Also, pay attention to:

1. Sensible parameters such as too much jumping, running, and overloading schedules, whatever the sport.

2. A history of particular injuries and problems, including muscle weakness, structural imbalances & poor biomechanics—all examples of potential issues.

3. The level of competition is always essential—young athletes should not be pushed over their heads too soon or too young.

4. Parents and coaches must listen closely to their young athletes' physical and mental pressures. These can lead to

problems that begin as relatively minor but then become persistent nightmares because the parents, coaches, or young athletes themselves refuse to back off and pay attention to my two favorite words: "INTELLIGENT REST!"

The extensive bottom line is for youth sports parents to be aware of these crucial factors—being active participants in their youngster's sports activities. Parents should accept and appreciate their responsibilities and communicate their concerns with their athletes' coaches. Try to remember my late sports psychology colleague Jim Vicory's key points: *"Be aware and informed. Don't be a critic. Enjoy the ride!"*

UNIVERSAL EXERCISES: WHATEVER THE SPORT

As a sports podiatrist, of course, I'm prejudiced. But the fact is that strengthening your feet and ankles is one of the most vital things you can do. It is crucial to maintaining balance.

It doesn't matter what sport, level, or age; all players have two fundamental goals: prevent injuries and enhance performance. We have stressed how youth sports injuries are at epidemic levels-especially overuse and repetitive motion injuries!

Ankle injuries remain one of the most common sports injuries. That alone is a good reason to focus on strengthening both feet and ankles, but it is not the only one. Strengthening feet and ankles can enhance speed, quickness, agility, and balance—crucial in all sports.

The feet and ankles are the body's base and foundation of support, but they are often neglected unless rehabilitating a previous injury. Strengthening and training these areas routinely and proactively makes much more sense.

Old routines usually involved tape or braces for ankles, which have a place but are generally for those with previously injured ankles or reoccurring problems. These can be helpful but fail to replace proper foot and ankle strengthening, which can benefit other areas like shins, knees, and back.

Winning The "Head" Game

Too often, we see young athletes concerned with how much they can bench press or work their arm and shoulder muscles- these are the "show muscles." But these same athletes might have difficulty balancing on one foot!

Foot and ankle strength and stability exercises are just as crucial for functional strength—the ability to move with power and speed, change direction, stop, and start with balance. Simple, inexpensive equipment like rubber bands and elastic tubing, balance boards, mini trams, and pieces like the innovative Sanddune Stepper are all helpful in strengthening the feet and ankles.

Balance work enhances knee, hip, core, and back stability and strength. Creating imbalance with unstable surfaces demands all our stabilizer muscles in our whole bodywork to gain and regain stability and balance (proprioception—where the body is in space). I (Dr. Bob) call these exercises *"Stability Training."*

Try balancing on one foot, standing on a trampoline, or tilting boards. It's challenging, safe, and fun! These stabilizers and small muscles help protect all the feet, ankles, knees, hips, and spine joints. Switching your feet changes the balance demands and functionally works different body areas.

Rubber bands and elastic tubing have always been one of the most effective ways to strengthen all the ranges of motion of our ankles. Moving the ankles up and down, side to side, in and out, can strengthen all the lower leg muscles and tendons. Slow, deliberate movements are best when using bands or tubing. They are available in different widths and resistances. Start light and move through a full range of motion. Work gradually.

Getting instructions on proper technique and progression from a physical therapist or athletic trainer is always helpful. These exercises are simple and safe for all ages and levels, but don't let their simplicity fool you—top athletes in all sports have significantly benefited from regular and intense use.

Always put off until tomorrow,
those things you shouldn't do at all.

THE PHYSICAL CHALLENGE

Over the years, I have seen many players with great physical tools and upside potential who had to be pushed to blossom. I genuinely believe a coach's essential role is to challenge players on who and where they are in their physical development and their capabilities in developing physicality in the future.

A lot of promise is just that for unpolished players with loads of potential who need to get stronger, stricter, and more durable. This transformation in my book begins in the workout room. Physicality in sports is initiated from the ground up. Any athlete will be hard-pressed to play effectively without strength in the feet, ankles, and legs.

Think about it: The ability to move quickly and efficiently depends on what happens at your base. Your base is imperative to developing the solid reactionary forces needed in sports acceleration and mobility. From this ground floor, you can extend the muscular structure and grit of the rest of the body.

When you work out regularly, your muscles build greater endurance for physical movement and activity. I have known players who were workout freaks. They would attack the most mundane and painful workouts as if they were a privilege.

It has been my experience that healthy-minded athletes moderate their indulgence. Follow me closely on this one: how you treat your body should be patterned on the rules of good health and well-being, not on pleasure or showmanship. The excellence and dignity of caring for yourself don't mean abandoning luxury and pleasurable living; do it in moderation.

For any young player, I would say to grasp that physicality is the route to a brighter future. Gain an incredible knowledge of how to develop your body, talents, and abilities. Become strict about working out and building on your strengths. Win the physical battle.

Chapter Sixteen

KNIT-TIGHT LOCKER ROOM

We firmly believe there is one thing that can further the mental readiness of a team before they step between the lines. That's the team leadership setting the stage for creating a knit-tight locker room. Leaders take a big step in this direction when establishing core team standards and principles to help guide everyone associated with the team. These standards and principles are not just words on a piece of paper but are well-thought-out and packed with meaning and significance.

From the back of the room, this question arises: *"What are core standards and principles, and why should a team have them?"*

First, they are preferences based on what is determined as the most desirable response in any situation. Every day in sports--and in life--athletes encounter problems that challenge them to decide what is right or wrong, good or bad, just or unjust, and even why they play sports. Some of these situations are unique; many are routine, and others are significant.

Almost everything a player does—every choice made, every action taken—is based on a system of standards and principles. These should be presented to all individuals who participate in team activities and events.

The answer to the second question is grounded in the fact that the core values are the principles established to guide actions and conduct from administrators to coaches to the water boy, even to parents and fans. These core values define proper behavior for those associated with the team. While they may not outline potential consequences for improper behavior, they form the basis for rules and regulations covering unsuitable conduct.

The team's core values give all members a keen sense of direction and focus. When the core values of a team have been clearly defined and implicitly and explicitly presented to the team, there is no guessing about what is expected.

Thinking and doing the right thing and valuing the established rules and regulations reflect the true spirit of professionalism, forming the foundation of a team's culture. A team develops an ingrained culture into its DNA by creating intentional and proactive core values. These values are the driving force in helping a team rely on each other as it strives to reach its full potential. A team with a quality culture can more readily adapt and adjust to conditions that aren't exactly how they were expected to go.

The critical step is identifying applicable team core values that best fit the team's character and makeup. Team values chosen wisely and discriminately by coaches and leaders provide direction, discipline, a relaxed atmosphere, and purpose in all the activities a team engages in regularly.

Our top ten core standards and principles for anyone associated with a team include (not in any particular order) Teamwork, Sportsmanship, Respect, Enthusiasm, Interactional skills, Diversity Sensitivity, Encouragement, Ego drive, the (Law of) Everything, and Fun. There are a ton of others you can choose from, but this is our list.

PERSONAL STANDARDS AND PRINCIPLES

The workable standards and principles employed by each individual are the key to creating and sustaining the team's culture. These standards and principles are best measured by their alignment with the team. The more closely aligned personal standards and principles are with the team, the easier it is for any player to function within the confines of the team's culture.

Personal standards and principles provide implications and sound direction for a team. However, these standards and principles move on beyond the playing field to reflect daily life behavior.

Winning The "Head" Game

It is essential to note that the extent of team core values is far beyond the players on the team. Significant situations and critical moments arise where the actions, conduct, and behavior of all administrators, coaches, management, and staff reflect core values.

Strictly from a player's standpoint, a player must apply these core values in playing situations, meeting fans, talking to media, on the practice field, in the dressing room, and when interacting with coaches and teammates. In our estimation, the key is to make the standards and principles count for something exceptional. Unless they are credible and concise, they are not worth the time and effort spent putting them together or talking about them.

TEAMWORK

> **Your emphasis as a teammate is being a great teammate. Regardless of how insignificant you may think your role is in the larger scheme of things—being a top-notch teammate serves you personally in two ways: It helps you counteract any self-defeating thoughts through your association with positively supportive people, and their encouraging words help you to confidently move forward in your quest to advance your athletic skills.**

Here are other thoughts on teamwork:

- There is no "I" in team.

- The term "team" has no meaning except the meaning given to each team member.

- WE always outplays ME.

- A real team has more 'we go' and less 'ego.'

- A team's strength is built around unity and a feeling of oneness.

- *"Teamwork-works,"* when each team member works.

- The more a team accomplishes, the less anyone should be concerned with who gets the credit.

- The main ingredient in being a star is the support given by the rest of the team.

- "The most valuable player on the team is the one who makes the most players valuable." -Peyton Manning

- A real team effort depends on everyone pushing up, not pulling down. The strength that team members give to each other will be there when it is needed.

- The team members who prefer to do it alone do not win nearly as much as those with the best TEAM players.

- *"None of us will ever be as good as all of us."*

-Selected from various sources

SPORTSMANSHIP

Pay attention to your thoughts. for they become beliefs...

Pay attention to your beliefs, for they become values...

Pay attention to your values, for they become attitudes...

Pay attention to your attitudes, for they become actions ...

Pay attention to your actions, for they become habits...

Pay attention to your habits, for they define character...

Pay attention to your character, for it forms your destiny.

-Adapted from an unknown source

Character and reputation are at the center of any display of sportsmanship. Character is what you are—your private substance. Reputation is what others think you are—your public image.

A reputation is a message about you that grows and travels by word of mouth. A reputation, however, is a fragile thing. Should you compromise on character, it can be easily fractured.

Upright and impeccable character is the only sound foundation for a solid reputation. The character of your play is based

Winning The "Head" Game

on your overall character. All that to say, *"Competition not only builds character, it reveals character."*

Later in this chapter, we discussed how integrity is at the heart of sportsmanship development. Integrity is the primary ingredient of character. It is a constant in building honesty and truthfulness. Integrity also resides at the very core of one's reputation. Integrity lays the foundation for sportsmanship.

In any form of athletics, sportsmanship has no peer. It is the lasting power of your desire to do the right thing. Get into your mind a clear picture of the kind of sportsman you want to be as a player. Then, act every time you play according to that image. Don't forget whatever choice you make serves to make you who you become.

Always be a beacon of sportsmanship. Answer with an unqualified "Yes," the challenge of doing what is right because it is right. It is not always going to be easy because, many times, you are going against the current. But that's the right direction. So, establish your course. Plant your feet. Build a foundation. Then, there will be no questions about how you will play.

We want to discuss one other issue: good sportsmanship. Sportsmanship doesn't come automatically or effortlessly to every young athlete, especially after a tough loss. We believe athletes must do these three things after every game: First, shake hands, trade high-fives or exchange fists, and tell the opposing team, "*Good game.*" This shows the opposing players that you respect and appreciate them.

Secondly, if your team has won, celebrate your victory, but don't stand around bragging, boasting, or making fun of the losing team. Nothing is earned by putting an opposing team down. It's okay to enjoy a win, but show respect for your opponent.

Thirdly, be courteous when you lose. You know you will not always end up on the winning side of the ledger. Take responsibility for your losses instead of bad-mouthing the other team or blaming the loss on something or someone else, notably the officials. Use these three tactics to guide your sportsmanship experiences.

A young player who is taught about sportsmanship learns a great deal that will be valuable in life: how the rules are made to be followed, how to play fair and square, how to be humble in victory, how to lose without becoming emotionally upset; and also, how to give a victorious opponent full credit. All these prepare you for living with integrity.

RESPECT

Respect is an essential component of both personal identity and relationships with those associated with the team. Respect can best be defined as esteem, honor, and a sense of the worth of someone or something.

Respect is the epitome of the way you treat others around you. It is what you want in return. Regarding team members and coaches, respect is a crucial aspect to the functionality of a team being united. To be a team—everyone has to be united as one. The epitome of respect is when all work together for the good of all.

We hope you understand that respect for others is fundamental. However, know that you will value others only to the extent you can appreciate yourself. As you increase your appreciation for your self-worth, you enhance your ability to receive value in return. Expanding your self-respect increases your potential value to the world around you. Wrap your hands around that component of truth!

You must understand that self-connection is the key to creating the confidence to bring a higher value to your external connections. When you feel truly confident in who you are, you interact with others on the team at a higher plane. When you positively honor yourself, the actual value will show in the way you approach coaches and teammates and how they approach you.

There's no question that the more you produce something remarkable in how you feel about yourself, the better the respect others have for you will be. This self-connection empowers you and makes you self-assured.

Winning The "Head" Game

Much of the material in this book is intended to elevate your self-respect. As your respect for yourself grows, so does your ability to value and honor your coaches' and teammates' words and actions. You will find yourself increasing the depths of your connections because you are becoming more trustworthy. That enhances your overall connectivity ability.

One final thought on respect before we move on. Possess the utmost respect for an opponent. The loss (or minus) column contains those who underestimated an opponent. Respect is an impeccable part of preparation leading up to and during the game. Just think, if you had no opposition, there would be no reason to play the game in the first place. Would that be possible?

ENTHUSIASM

Playing sports calls for a high-intensity level and full-fledged flow of adrenaline if you are to be successful at it. While involvement in the action is essential, it means little without performing with an intense level of enthusiasm.

Where does enthusiasm come from? It arises from excitement and a strong interest in what you are doing. It is a potent tool for generating the vitality needed to sustain action. Enthusiasm can create an overall feeling of well-being with many worthwhile side effects, such as energy, willpower, and fearlessness.

You can rarely play uniquely without enthusiasm in your playbook. Enthusiasm is one of those things that gives you a chance to have a sustaining relationship with success. Your effort will remain high if it is part of your activity level.

Just for the record, happiness is based on enthusiasm. Being happy about what you do emanates from being enthused about doing it. Think about that for a moment.

Enthusiasm is like any other worthwhile attribute. It is the result of conscious effort. Because it rarely comes naturally, enthusiasm must first be generated internally, then continually practiced and nurtured.

It is essential to understand that while enthusiasm is an individual thing, it is never purely a personal matter, for it affects personal efforts and significantly positively affects others. In that regard, be the captain of enthusiasm on your team.

"ENTHUSIASM defies the laws of mathematics,
for when you divide it, it multiplies."
-Tom Peters

Without Enthusiasm...

All that you know is incomplete.
All that you think is insufficient.
All that you believe is insignificant.
All that you do is inadequate.

*Be the captain on your team
in charge of enthusiasm!*

INTERACTIONAL SKILLS

We see interactional skills, or lack thereof, as one of the biggest challenges facing the development of team togetherness. The inherent inclusion of the ability to effectively communicate and interact is an essential value on a team. However, it may be an illusion and somewhat vague to many.

Effective communication is vital to collaborative behavior among all team members. All team members need to understand and appreciate that effective communication allows everyone to engage successfully with a pattern of relational and interactional skills. These skills include listening, asking questions, tone of voice, and word use.

Interactional skills are established and time-honored when you regularly create a reciprocal mutuality with team members. Words, listening, actions, and unspoken expressions of care and concern accompany this mutuality. Being interactively savvy is essential when establishing positive relations with those around you

Winning The "Head" Game

who share a standard team purpose. This first-hand reality requires the transparent exchange of information, sharing of ideas, and significant opportunities for building solid team connections and individual relationships.

Much of the interaction between people today is transmitted with two fingers on an electronic device, for better or worse. Social media has many benefits, such as the way of communicating and interacting, that permeate today's society. Significant pitfalls are also detrimental to building a solid relational base that is so important to team interaction. On behalf of all, collective interactional efforts add a measurable sense of permanency to what goes on in a locker room.

Reflect for a moment on what is going on in your locker room. How deeply rooted in the breadth and depth of your relationships with teammates? How is the team doing to develop and build more profound and visibly meaningful personal relationships?

The quest to be social is innate to human character. Human nature craves human interaction, and technology cannot effectively replace it. While technology will continue to grow as time passes, the value of personal friendships and relationships will play a key role in ensuring a team's success in the future. Our take is that quality relationships between yourself, other team members, and coaches are essential to team chemistry.

Set a goal of consistently communicating and interacting with as many of your teammates as possible. A great way to do this is to improve the quality of your listening. This will, in turn, improve your ability to connect and interact with others.

Our Maker was telling us something when He gave us two ears and only one mouth! There is little doubt that developing communication skills starts with your ears, not your mouth. To get to know people better, listen to them better. You can learn a lot about an individual simply by listening to understand the conversation and the message being conveyed better. As Yogi Berra astutely said, *"You can see a lot by listening."*

Team relationships are created, nurtured, and developed with expectations to grow and improve the *"togetherness"* vital to a team's success. These relationships cannot be manufactured, designed, or forced. They are established when you create the right interactional skills and a climate to grow and cultivate them.

DIVERSITY SENSITIVITY

We can tell you that diversity is an essential concern on a team today. We considered putting the diversity issue under the previous heading on interactional skills, but it is too important not to assign a separate title.

Diversity extends far beyond race or ethnic group. It encompasses age, personality, background, speech style, and more. Most sports teams are made up of players from different cultural backgrounds. Showing sensitivity, treating others as equals, being flexible, and striving to find creative ways to work through cultural barriers have as much to do with team unity as anything. Each team member is laden with the responsibility to make this a priority.

Developing respect for a diverse group of people is a highly valued quality in building team chemistry. Everyone should have the right to be different and respect that difference. Extreme differences can be positive because they create a unique identity. Since individual differences exist, every team member needs to understand that everyone associated with a team is due respect for the fact of who they are.

Do you hear us saying that you owe your teammates fundamental respect, even if you do not approve of or share everything they do? Respecting others does not mean judging them by their attitudes, behavior, or thoughts. It means accepting them as individuals and all the power the word "individual" carries with it.

The ever-present challenges on a diverse team bring authenticity and the influence of esteem to the forefront. Continue to upgrade all aspects of the challenges embedded in diversity. Continue to grow convincingly in respect for all team members.

ENCOURAGEMENT

A given in sports is to experience mental and psychological pain of some kind and degree at times. Past disappointments and hurts that many have learned to cover with false smiles and cheerful actions exist inside fortresses of insulation. Those who experience this pain have built solid emotional walls to protect themselves. Maybe you have been right where they are. We have been there.

Around you, on occasion, are teammates who need to be comforted and consoled. For a teammate who is hurting, you can convey a message of support and bonding that can make positive deposits into that person's emotional account. One of the nicest things you can give to a teammate is something to feel important about. There is not a better way to solidify a relationship.

So, if a teammate or team member is not performing as well as they are capable of performing. What can you do? Be a leader and take the initiative to move, excite, and uplift those who need encouragement. Help them focus their energies and desires by offering a positive message. Inspire them to believe that what they want is attainable. Appeal to their reasoning, but more importantly, stir their emotions.

In those times when things are uncertain and production is at a standstill, most of your teammates need a few words of assurance, a little compassion, and much encouragement. They need a team leader to breathe fresh fire into their fading embers. They need a leader who tells them their efforts will improve their productivity. They need a team leader who can stoke the fire.

But your role is not always just for those with obvious signs of discomfort. Often, the less obvious shared glances and unspoken thoughts are from those seeking comfort for troubled hearts and hidden fears. There are countless teammates all around you who are desperately hungry for someone to offer a kind word. They are looking for an encourager. That sounds like you.

Encouraging one teammate may not change the team chemistry today, but your words of encouragement may change that teammate's world forever. Often, a word of praise, expression of thanks, or show of appreciation may make a difference for that one teammate. Take time to help bring out the best in a teammate...the best that might spur that teammate on to new heights of possibilities.

How about the teammates that you see around you who are hurting? Do you offer them a caring ear when one is needed? The one thing that they do not need is another critic. They hurt enough. They don't need more "do this" or "do that."

They need support. They need someone to walk beside them. They need to experience the warmth of a heart and be blessed by words that mean something...the kind that sinks in. Blessed are those who speak words of encouragement.

Please Encourage Me

> Often, we see others here and there,
> With faces that are filled with grief;
> And we know that a comforting word,
> Might bring them much-needed relief.
> But do we offer them a single-word
> To help make their way more bright?
> Do we speak tender reassuring words
> To provide them with a source of light?
> Every uplifting word offered to another
> Is what to the earth is sun and rain;
> Never was an encouraging word wasted,
> Never was one given to another in vain.
> Author unknown

EGO DRIVE

There is a saying that goes: *"We need more we go and less ego."* Would it surprise you to discover that the best way to have more *"we go"* is to have a strong *"ego drive and ego strength?"*

First, it is wise to understand that ego drive differs from ego-driven. The latter person looks out for their self-interest...

regardless. People with a strong ego drive have a purpose—a 'why'—outside themselves that drives them to do what they do.

In our estimation, ego drive refers to a particular need to achieve—a means of gaining satisfaction from wanting and needing to do a good job personally—for themselves and the team. Those with great empathy and a strong ego drive put themselves in a position to interact with teammates more successfully. Possessing empathy and ego drive is not a contradiction—quite the contrary.

Those with good empathy but too little ego drive tend to experience ineffectiveness with more demanding individuals. When the *heat is on*, these individuals are more likely to use sympathy than empathy. Since they do not thrive on *standing their ground*, they find a more leisurely route and give in. Instead of an adequate compromise, they feel *sorry* for someone and give in. The lack of ego drive ends up hurting them in the end.

Ego strength is needed to bounce back after dealing with a difficult situation that did not end well. This is especially true in sports of any kind. It is often required after a tough loss.

Egos can become weak and adversely affect both present and future relationships. Ego strength is a trigger— a motivation to keep going when the inner spirits would instead turn tail and run. Minus the bounce-back ability supplied by ego strength, most people find themselves on an emotional roller coaster.

To recap, those with little ego strength may feel torn between the competing demands of others. Those with too much ego strength can become too unyielding and rigid with others. Striking a balance is the key. You will interact well with various people if you possess empathy, a strong ego drive, and worthy ego strength.

EVERYTHING (LAW OF)

> **The Law of 'Everything' reads:** *"Everything you do matters. There is no neutrality. For every choice, there is a consequence. It will either add value to your career or it won't".*

Most of our significant choices begin with our attitudes about the circumstances surrounding those choices. The fast-paced action of athletics leads to ample choices that carry many consequences. For that reason, success in athletics—as in life—finds its footing in everything we do through choices and, ultimately, consequences.

The results of anything you do will be determined by the type of choices you make while performing your duties. Some choices carry more weight than others, but no choice is inconsequential during an athletic contest. Every choice you make leads you inexorably to either advance or weaken the execution of your role or, in a broader sense, the overall role of team-related activities.

When you cut right to the heart of every game or match situation, there must be some choice about an opponent's choice…and there will be a consequence. For example, a baseball pitcher must decide what pitch to throw. Hidden deep behind that decision are the hitter's attitude, the ball/strike count, and game situation. The consequence of the pitch is an outcome of the choice made by the pitcher, not the catcher.

Buy into this choice/consequence concept and its role in sports and life. Embedded deeply in your psyche should be the reality that there is a consequence in every choice you make. Some of these choices are inherently more meaningful than others. Some choices also will affect your life more than others. Whenever you face two very different options, your choice will likely impact one area more than others. That's an important principle to understand.

In the bigger scheme of things, please don't lose sight of the fact that the consequence determines what happens, but the choice sets the table. The outcomes will instinctively differ as you gain more experience in making better choices. Repetition. The right repetition. It leads to more quality choices and consequences.

Make the right choices to enhance your future. Here's a choice that we recommend: Get a running start and jump right on to a bright future… You might just be surprised at the stunning and exciting place where you land.

FUN

Surprised? That's right. No fancy title here: Every team member needs to have fun. Why do something if you fail to enjoy and have fun at it?

Sports participation can be very intense and demanding, lessening the joy you can receive from involvement. Unless you find something within the sports experience to revitalize your spirit and make you feel great on the inside for doing it, you will be hard-pressed to play at a championship level.

Undoubtedly, the ability to sustain motivation comes from loving what you do and the enjoyment you receive from being a team member and interacting with others. The drive required to perform any task effectively is more readily accessible through the power generated from the energy of interacting with teammates. Experiencing celebratory occasions and successes enhances the delight and pleasure that come from team participation.

Having fun is vital to success in any sports activity. Here are some essential benefits of this role.

- Provides perspective
- Enhances the ability to adapt
- Enhances interest
- Increases productivity
- Defuses stress

A SONNY MOMENT

How important is a team culture built around impeccable team standards and principles? Ask this question of any Hall of Fame coach, and your answer will probably differ for each one. To answer this question, this is crucial to developing team unity.

I think a coach's most enormous task and greatest joy is to see his players mature, grow as human beings, and become productive members of society. A coach lives consciously for himself, but unconsciously he serves as an instrument for the achievement of those around him. I don't know who said it, but this quote fits right in with what I am talking about: *"Let your light shine so brightly that those around you who stand in the darkness will be illuminated by the light of who you really are."*

Another critical aspect of coaching is earning the respect of those around you. I don't believe a coach can gain respect unless he is consistent. If a coach always did different things in similar circumstances, the word consistency would not come to mind as appropriate. A coach who constantly assumes a different perspective and changes the thought process keeps those around him guessing what comes next. Little good can come from something based on unexpected changes and inconsistencies.

Two things shape and make a great team: balance and harmony. Balance deals more with the physical side of things, while harmony is more of an emotional/behavioral factor.

Balance begins with having a team with the right mindset concerning overall team strategy and tactics. Then, a coaching staff's challenge is to offset a team's unequal abilities by assisting those with lesser abilities to work at practice and maximize their strengths. In this regard, everyone on the team is assured they will possess the skills to allow them to compete for playing time.

Balance makes for a better team. When every player works hard to improve themselves and pushes their teammates to do the same, the results are more significant. Striking for balance never hurts...but it can certainly help.

Harmony creates a culture of togetherness. No one wants to play in a toxic environment. Harmony sets the foundation for future success by creating a culture where everyone feels good about their role and responsibility.

The message is plain: players and coaches alike need to blend in. We all know teamwork and working together as a unit are critical components in successful teams. However, that doesn't mean there are no disagreements and elements of friction in a team.

A spirit of harmony means that teammates and coaches work through those moments and seek collaborative solutions when the locker room plays host to turmoil and disorder.

Finally, I want to say a few words about leadership. Blessed are those who are leaders. Strong leadership is needed to turn team goals into reality. In my estimation, the best leaders on a team are the ones who lead by example. However, effective leadership also depends on utilizing good communication skills.

The thing is, it's not simple to develop leaders. All the great team leaders I had over the years had one thing in common: they directly impacted the team's success and ability to deliver results. You can't develop a winning team without having the right talent—including leaders—on the roster.

Some believe great leaders are born, while others believe they are made. The truth is that no manual or guide will give a player all the tricks to become a great leader. Being a leader comes through the maturation of wisdom, which generally comes through experience and maturity. At least, that has been my experience.

The bottom line is those players who are leaders play a critical role in the success of any team. These leaders have a great ability to steer and encourage others toward common goals. Blessed be the leaders who lead.

Chapter Seventeen

EPILOGUE

Winning the "head" game is a personal choice. It makes little difference where you are in your development right now. What is important is the great discovery you have made about yourself as we have journeyed through the book together and the gigantic steps you have already taken toward realizing your potential. Genuinely, we believe this is the beginning of a new ending for you. We celebrate that you are ready to go.

Over these years, we have discovered that the growth opportunities presented to you as an athlete become more prevalent the more actively you create and pursue them. Some of these opportunities come from experience, some from experimenting, some from example, some from making errors, and some from unexpected places. But they all come when you are energetic and enthusiastically hustling to find those "unexpected places."

So, as you prepare to leave us and ride from what you are today to seek what you will become tomorrow, the mystery and adventure of the journey are in great hands—your own. Keep training, Keep practicing. Keep hustling. Keep improving. But also keep this book close at hand. Whether in sports—or life—this book can serve as an authentic reference source for your future. The nature of this book requires the gift of presence. It demands the gift of action. Up to it?

APPENDIX
(WALLSTUFF)

ALL ABOUT WINNING

Winning is the bottom line. It is why you go through all the preparatory things presented in the previous chapters. In sports, there are always winners and losers. We believe winning plays a vital role in becoming a fully integrated athlete—and provides a track you can run on as you tackle whatever life presents and do it on your terms.

This chapter offers many reminders about why winning is so important. These are the kinds of things you can copy and put in a place where they can constantly remind you. Don't let anyone tell you that your human drive to win will be anything but crucial. Sports and life are all about creating a winning culture.

One of the givens of athletics is constantly meeting a new opponent who brings a new challenge. The significance of moving on to the next opportunity with continual momentum requires a richer recognition of looking forward with anticipation, not backward with celebratory reflection.

"Winning may not be everything… but it does
beat anything that finishes in second place."
Paul (Bear) Bryant

High achievers never confuse movement with progress. They stay focused on finding the resources they need to activate successful results that will move the needle.

*Winning is not everything, but it
beats anything that comes in second.*

WINNING COMES FROM...

WINNING comes from a Challenge..........accept it.

WINNING comes from an Adventure............dare it.

WINNING comes from an Opportunity..........take it.

WINNING comes from a Mystery…….........unfold it.

WINNING comes from being Demanding.......face it.

WINNING comes from tackling a Puzzle.......solve it.

WINNING comes from taking a Risk.....undertake it.

WINNING comes from reaching a Goal.....achieve it.

WINNING comes from an Experience….…....enjoy it.

WINNING comes from a Mission…...……...fulfill it.

WINNING comes from a Mindset……..…develop it.

"Winners never take time to learn the meaning of defeat."
-General James Mathis

WANT TO WIN?

If a team wants to WIN...

Believes it can WIN...

Prepares itself to WIN...

Sees itself WINNING...

Commits itself to WINNING...

Performs like a WINNER...

Then what beyond itself is there

To keep it from winning?

**Winners' realize winning is
not everything, but striving to win is.**

ANATOMY OF WINNERS

Winners have a badge of honor for doing their best... giving the most they have...and enjoying peak productivity.

Winners mentally paint big pictures and then work to turn those pictures into reality.

Winners set stretch goals and work relentlessly toward making them a reality.

Winners adopt a code of conduct that sets high standards of thought and behavior and holds these standards sacred—without succumbing to pressure to change them.

Winners desire things from themselves as well as desire things for themselves. They believe that to receive something, they must give something... and the giving of themselves always comes first.

Winners recognize that winning is something they experience on the inside, not something they have on the outside. It is measured by what they hold in their hearts, not their hands.

Winners are always thankful for what they have and then set out to do their best to improve it.

Winners believe that to count for something special to others, you must first count for something special to yourself.

Winners move forward as if the limits of what they are capable of doing do not exist.

Winners carry the feeling that they are doing what their hearts desire... and doing it well.

Winners appreciate that winning is important—otherwise, why would anyone hand out blue ribbons?

-Adapted from numerous sources

> ### WINNING IS ABOUT RESULTS
>
> Winning is not about how you look, even though how you look can help you feel like a winner.
>
> Winning is not about your knowledge level–although you couldn't perform well without it.
>
> Winning is not about the skills you acquire- even though your skill set contributes significantly to winning.
>
> Winning is not about how you perform – even though your performance is vital to winning.
>
> Winning is about results…the kind of results you want happen over time, not overnight, but the questions are these: Did you get the desired results? Did you make it to the podium to receive the trophy?
>
> -Unknown source

"I can be a winner" is the vision.
"I'll work to be a winner" is the price.
"I will be a winner" is the ticket.
"I am a winner" is the prize.
-Adapted from an unknown source

"Champions do their best in less critical situations, so they will respond with a higher impulse in more critical situations."
-Jim Rone

"If you believe in yourself, have dedication and pride, and never quit, you'll be a winner. The price of victory is high – but so are the rewards."
-Paul (Bear) Bryant

Winning indicates you have
played the game the right way.

Winning The "Head" Game

WHAT WINNERS' DO

Winners proceed as if the limits to their capabilities do not exist…they are always attempting to make something happen… sitting back and waiting is not their trademark.

Winners create circumstances, not victims of circumstances. They are not trapped by routine. They do not cling to the familiar when something better is within reach.

Winners recognize that they are not accomplishing much else if they do not make a few mistakes along the way.

Winners realize that it is impossible to win at a high level without staring losing in the eye and risk trying to win.

Winners work on the theory that if you accept the risk of losing, the odds of winning will work in your favor.

Winners see that the more exposure they have to winning opportunities, the more likely they will succeed.

Winners don't worry about failing… they think about the chances they miss if they fail to attempt.

Winners believe it will be challenging to be good at anything they do unless they attempt to be good at everything.

Winners live with the supportive feeling that they will always strive to make something happen. Around a winners' locker room, that attitude counts for something very special.

-Unknown source

"High achievers never confuse movement with progress. They stay focused on finding the resources they need to activate successful movement that will move the needle."
-Larry D. Thornton

Sonny Smith and Lou Vickery

ROUTE TO VICTORY

If you appreciate that there is something better than you have ever experienced in sports...

If you have strong feelings about what you are doing... and work through your doubts and fears...

If you concern yourself with your performance and focus on what you must do...

If you always try to do your best at practice or in a game...

If you discipline yourself to stay the course even when the odds are stacked against your team...

If you want to succeed badly enough and patiently work toward making daily improvements...

If you keep your focus on the present and do not let yesterday or tomorrow weigh you down...

If you are courageous enough to risk making things happen when things need to happen...

If you take the initiative to grow beyond your difficulties and meet your challenges head on...

If you follow your dreams and desires to excel...

If you work hard and smart to maximize your physical resources...

If you tie a knot and hold on when you feel you are at the end of your rope...

If in the far reaches of your heart, you truly believe you have what it takes to be a winner...

The odds are in your favor to emerge as the victor in the greatest contest of all – the contest with yourself.

-Adapted from several sources

BEING NUMBER ONE...

First and foremost, commit to being the best athlete possible.

Have a clear direction—not scattered vision--of where you are going and why you want to go that way.

Possess discipline and self-mastery to distance yourself from intolerance and over-indulgence in things that harm the body, mind, and soul.

Prepare yourself with an education and acquire expertise that will set you above the crowd.

Realize that there is only one option when it comes to the process of success—being committed to it. In-between is not an option.

Appreciate that the results obtained directly reflect your best effort to honor the coaches' process for success.

Demonstrate leadership that prompts others to accept and follow your direction and actions readily.

Being number one is making the decision that you will always attempt to come through...every moment you participate.

-Selected from numerous sources

"Winning is a validation; it means all of the sweat, hustle, practice time, playing hard and smart has paid off."
-Jimmy Johnson

"A team removes a big roadblock to winning when it learns there is a big difference between doing something and getting something done."
-Steve Spurrier

Winners do not concern themselves with non-essential stuff, because most of it is non-essential.

STEPS TO BEING A WINNER

Dream more than most think is practical…
Expect more than most think is wise…
Prepare better than most think is possible…
Risk more than most think is feasible…
Do more than most think is worthy…
and keep on doing it.
-Source unknown

The secret to winning is found inward -- not outward.

WINNING FORMULA

Keep your THOUGHTS positive,
Because your THOUGHTS become
 your ACTIONS.
Keep your ACTIONS positive…
Because your ACTIONS become
 your HABITS.
Keep your HABITS positive,
Because your HABITS become
 your PERFORMANCE BASE.
Keep your PERFORMANCE BASE
 strong and current.
Because your PERFORMANCE BASE
 becomes your WINNING FORMULA.
-Adapted from an unknown author

ACKNOWLEDGMENTS

An undertaking of this type and size requires the involvement of countless people. We would like to give a shout-out to those who took the time and effort to help us make this a reality.

Not only did many of those asked to provide a review do just that, but they took the time to do some editing and offer some sage recommendations.

Then there is Rich Kozak. Rich is my brand mentor. He jumped all over this project with his editing pin. It's incredible how some people can find the misuse of a word or usage of an improper tense that escaped the editor. Rich's forty-plus years in writing and editing were a valuable, if not surprising, assistance.

We thank Denny Kearley, Priscilla Wilder, and Wendall Walker for their valuable input and use of an editing pen.

We especially thank Shannon Castello (and Rich) for designing the beautiful cover. Shannon also offered her usual insightful commentary about the book's content.

We thank anyone we have overlooked. It was not intentional. Your encouragement, criticism, patience, and, most of all, tremendous support were often timely and much needed.

Winning The "Head" Game

Made in the USA
Columbia, SC
27 October 2024